Not Just Another Vendor

About the Author

Nigel Cullington
Nigel serves as VP of Marketing for
Upland Software's Sales Effectiveness division
UplandSoftware.com/Altify

About the Co-Authors

Zoë Randolph
Zoë is a writer and researcher who covers history,
culture, and business
ZoeRandolph.com

Paulo Sellitti
Paulo is the founder of Hypnotic Design,
a strategic storytelling consultancy
HypnoticDesign.com

NOT JUST ANOTHER VENDOR

How top sales leaders use
Account Planning to build trust
and grow revenue

Nigel Cullington

·OAK·TREE·PRESS·

Published by Oak Tree Press,
Cork T12 XY2N, Ireland.
www.OakTreePress.eu
www.SuccessStore.com

ISBN: 978-1-78119-557-4   Paperback
ISBN: 978-1-78119-558-1   PDF
ISBN: 978-1-78119-559-8   ePub
ISBN: 978-1-78119-560-4   Kindle

A catalogue record of this book is available
from the British Library.

Cover and story design by
Hypnotic Design
www.HypnoticDesign.com

Upland Altify
401 Congress Ave. #1850
Austin, TX 78701
www.UplandSoftware.com/Altify

Our Contributors

This book was made possible by the many sales leaders and subject-matter experts who graciously offered both their time and expertise to this project. Thank you!

Todd Adair
Southeast Zone
Commercial Manager,
GE Healthcare

Sarah Bennett
Vice President,
Global Finance and
Revenue Operations,
Informatica

Eric Chapman
Vice President, Sales
Operations and
Enablement,
Hexagon ALI

Jason Cooper
Head of Sales
Excellence,
Johnson Controls

Tim Foster
Director, Growth
Success, Capita

Alison Greenwood
Regional Vice
President and
General Manager -
SoCal, Media and
Entertainment,
Lumen

Travis Hill
Managing Director,
Strategic Consulting,
Upland Altify

Scott Jackson
Senior Director,
Sales Enablement,
Comcast Business

Billy Martin
Senior Director,
Leadership
Development and
Strategic Enablement
Programs,
Medidata

Eddie Pyrtle
Sales Coach,
Qlik Technologies

Anthony Reynolds
Chief Executive
Officer, HireVue

Pat Reilly
Senior Director, Sales
Field Enablement,
Medidata

Phil Trapani
Principal Consultant,
Upland Altify

Sarah Walker
Managing Director,
Enterprise,
Cisco

Table of Contents

Preface

What Great Looks Like

What separates a great sales organization from the merely good?

Objectively, they're not hard to recognize. Their win rates are higher. Their deals are bigger. Their sales cycles are faster. Their customers reliably come back for more.

What's less immediately obvious, though, is how the best do what they do.

How do they win more, win bigger, win faster?

How do they earn the kind of customer trust most sellers can only dream of?

I've worked with sales leaders and their teams for more than 25 years. Again and again, I've seen that success is built, not bought. Revenue isn't the product of a few star sellers, a fool-proof sales methodology, or silver-bullet sales software.

How, then, do the best separate themselves from the pack?

Simply put, exceptional sales organizations make their customers' goals the number one priority. These teams never ask "What can I sell?" Rather, they wonder, "What do our customers need to achieve and how can we help them get there?"

Note that I use the word "we" intentionally. Because the only way to truly put customers at the center of what you do is to rally the extended revenue team—from sellers to customer success, marketing, and beyond—and focus its collective energy on making real things happen.

It's this kind of radical reorientation that scores the ultimate win: relationships. When revenue teams put sustained success above individual sales, they start to earn the kind of trust that wins not only the deals in front of them but also the opportunity to defend and grow their position over the long term.

At Upland Altify, we call this approach "account planning." (You may have heard it referred to as "account-based selling," "outcome-based selling," or something else entirely.) Whatever you call it, account planning is rooted in the doctrine of mutually assured success. When your customers win, you win. In some ways, it's as simple as that.

Of course, if the practice of account planning was as easy to implement as the concept is to understand, we wouldn't have taken the time to write this book. But we did, because the truth of the matter is that account planning often fails. And usually it fizzles because leaders charge ahead without the tools and knowledge they need to make a lasting impact. Why?

Which hurdles trip teams up? How do some organizations manage to stay upright? How can you use account planning to reliably grow pipeline and close more opportunities?

Rather than attempt to answer these questions ourselves, we chose to take you straight to the source. We conducted hours of interviews with the world's top-performing sellers, coaches, and leaders to get to the heart of how account planning comes together—and how it falls apart.

This book is a compilation of these stories and a distillation of the lessons we can all take from them. It's an up-close look at what it takes to bring account planning to your organization, reorient the mindset of your extended revenue team, and move your sales performance from good to great. It's a sales leader's—or aspiring leader's—guidebook to winning the promotion, blazing past targets, and building a coalition of customers who see you as a trusted advisor, not just another vendor.

We'll get you there in *three* parts.

In **Part I**, we'll see exactly how account planning can transform your relationships and grow your pipeline.

In **Part II**, we'll prepare you to conquer the pitfalls that doom account planning so that you're ready to go all in with confidence.

In **Part III**, we'll get into the weeds and break down everything you'll need to construct your own approach tailored to your business.

These pages won't be filled with vague theories or self-congratulatory heroes' tales. Instead, they'll zero in on the kind of information you actually need: real experiences and best practices from the people who know what it takes.

Nigel Cullington
VP of Marketing, Upland Altify

Part I

Return on Account Planning

"We've been doing business with you for years.
Why are you just now asking about my business?"

Todd Adair, MHCL
Southeast Zone Commercial Manager,
GE Healthcare

1

The Trusted Advisor

Todd Adair has spent nearly 30 years in healthcare sales, 25 of them with GE Healthcare. Over his career, he's led go-to-market strategies, a global expansion of outcome selling across top strategic account teams, and the acceleration of commercial execution in top accounts across the US and Canada. He is currently the Commercial Manager for the Southeast Zone.

In 2014, sales leaders at GE Healthcare formed a new hypothesis about how sellers might perform better. The idea went something like this: if sellers thought more holistically about their customers and spent more time getting to the root of what each one was trying to achieve, teams would be better able to build the kinds of relationships that would pay off over the long term. In short, the theory was that being more than just another vendor made good business sense.

The concept was, in many respects, a doubling down on the sales ethos that had permeated the company as a whole for several years. Everyone knew that if GE wanted to remain an industry powerhouse, they'd have to put their customers at the center of their efforts. But despite widespread agreement that the sales approach needed an upgrade, little had materially changed.

Naturally, no self-respecting scientific company is content to accept unproven musings. The hypothesis needed to be put to the test. Would shifting sellers' focus away from the immediacy of closing deals actually drive more revenue? Or would the more nebulous goal of understanding their customers just end up muddying the waters?

GE Healthcare's sales leaders put their heads together. "We can push these ideas much further than we have in the past, and we need to get smarter about it," the group agreed. Together, they devised an experiment: they would pour their attention into 20 accounts across the globe, which would vary from massive healthcare systems to university medical centers. Then, they'd see how these accounts performed.

A pilot program was born, powered by a new sales technology implemented to help drive account planning best practices.

When veteran seller Todd Adair heard about the new pilot, he volunteered to participate without a second thought. It wasn't that he was itching to change his current selling approach, per se. Todd is simply the kind of person who always seizes the opportunity to learn something new. "I think my DNA just tells me that if there's a better way to do something, I want to try it," he says. "So I raised my hand and told them I'd be willing to put in the additional time and effort if it meant I could possibly get better."

Todd had been with GE for more than 15 years, but jumping into the unknown was how he'd built his career. In the summer after his junior year of college, unsure of what he wanted to do with his life, he found himself in the middle of Oklahoma with a gig selling books door to door—without a car. "I rode a bike all summer hauling a bag of books with me," remembers Todd, not without fondness.

What for others might have been three months of sweat and drudgery was for Todd an invigorating experience. Despite the heat and the hard work, he emerged with clarity about his future. "I knew at the end of that summer that selling was where I wanted to be," he says.

Joining GE Healthcare was the natural merging of his head and his heart. The son of a nurse, Todd grew up with an up-close view of the healthcare industry and believed deeply in doing his part to maximize its force in the world. His passion and skills made him a natural. By the time he asked to join the new customer-centric pilot program, Todd was already an accomplished seller who oversaw large teams that worked in major accounts.

He had been on the account in question for seven years and managed a team of 40 reps dedicated to it. The account was large and complex. His team didn't win all of the opportunities they competed for within it, "but," remembers Todd, "I certainly won my unfair share across the board, so I felt like I was doing a good job."

And by all objective measures, he was doing well. The account reliably brought in between $40–50 million every year.

"They were accustomed to buying from us," says Todd. "Obviously there was competition out there, but I was showing up on a frequent basis, and they were saying, "Yes." From my perspective, I figured, well, they're buying from me, right? They're giving me their business. So they must be getting the value they need."

But as the pilot program got underway, a new set of questions landed on Todd's desk. Instead of reporting on revenue numbers and deal progress, he was asked to gather insights at a level he'd never before attempted.

Todd had always considered himself well-versed in the particulars of his accounts. He knew when they budgeted. He knew how much money they had to spend. He knew all the things that would have earned him an A+ in Sales 101.

But the longer he spent considering things from the customer's point of view, the wider he could see the gap growing between how much he thought he knew and how much he actually did.

"What I didn't truly understand at the time was, well, *why?* Why are they budgeting that amount? Why are they replacing that piece of technology today? Why not last year? Why not in three years? I'd never been trained to ask those types of questions."

Like many veteran sellers, Todd had gone through his fair share of sales training. He'd studied Spin and Miller Heiman; he'd become a top-notch negotiator. But in most companies, he remembers, "They'd bring us in and tell us: 'here's everything that we have and why it's so great.' But they'd leave out the most important thing: the customer and what was important to *them.*"

So for years, Todd had, in his own telling, "fit the mold of a vendor." He knew his products inside and out, which, at a massive and complex company like GE Healthcare, was no small thing. "But when I walked in the door, they knew I was there to sell something. They knew the conversation was going to be about me and my stuff."

Now, it was time to flip the script.

"A lot of work went into the front end simply to understand the account," says Todd. He began devoting more and more time to seeking out deeper conversations, chasing people down, and convincing them to take the time out of their overflowing calendars to talk through exactly what his customer was trying to do. And as one of the first people in the company to attempt this new way of working, Todd had no playbook to follow. "We were building the plane while flying it," he says.

What he *did* have was a guiding vision: to develop an in-depth understanding of his customer and help them reach their goals.

As he took the time to ask better questions, a new world of potential insights began to unfold in the periphery of Todd's vision. He started thinking deeply about what his customer's goals were, how they were prioritizing projects, and how each of these insights fit into a wider vision for the future.

Armed with a more inquisitive approach, Todd began to ask the kinds of questions he'd never thought relevant to his efforts before. He invested more time in having conversations for the sake of understanding, not advancing a sale. He began to think beyond the walls separating his particular slice of GE to consider how his company as a whole might be able to help.

"I stopped approaching our conversations from a vendor-client perspective," says Todd. "Instead, I came with a curiosity mindset. I told them, help me understand your business better. You may not be using my technology today, but I'm not here to talk about that. I'm here to talk about *you*."

At first, the customer wasn't sure what to make of his new persona. "Their reaction," he recalls, "was shock."

"We've been doing business with you for years," one leader finally exclaimed, saying out loud what everyone in the room was thinking. "Why are you just now asking about *my* business?"

Now it was Todd's turn for shock.

"You should have been doing this all along," the leader continued. "But you haven't."

It was a gut punch. But like any good salesperson, Todd is more adept than the average person at bouncing back. "It was a very vulnerable moment," he admits. "But their reaction fueled a fire in me. I knew at that instant that I was onto something. Now, I needed to learn even more."

He charged forward, doubling down on his new approach. "'Partner' is an overused term, but considering myself one allowed me to think differently about my customer and realize that, if I could help solve their problems, I'd put myself in a much better spot."

And that's exactly what he did. Day after day, Todd showed up and listened. For nearly a year, he came with the express intent of understanding what people were up against and how he could help them chart a path forward. He was there when they were using his competitor. He was there as they held tight to a valued incumbent. As long as he thought he could help, Todd showed up.

"The biggest change for me was that I started trying to identify problems," he says. "I stopped being afraid to go in and sit down with key stakeholders and just say, 'Hey, here's your business as I understand it. Do I have that right?'"

In other words, Todd began to prioritize validating what he understood to be his customers' priorities. "It was one thing to have the discussion, but it was another thing to have a literal document—a piece of paper—that I could bring in that showed explicitly how I saw their business," he says. "This kind of visual, physical insight map took a lot more work, but it was a game changer."

"Wow," said his contracts the first time Todd placed an insight map on the table. "You really understand our business if you'll go to these lengths."

The more he showed up, the more new deals seemed to materialize before his eyes. "During these validation discussions, I'd learn about new opportunities I might not have caught wind of in the past because I hadn't been there asking the right questions," says Todd.

Those opportunities soon bore fruit. Todd and his team started winning deals they'd never won in the past.

"I went from sitting across the table from my customer to sitting on the same side. Now, the people across the table were the patients and the community members whom we were now working together to serve."

Before his customer's eyes, Todd had transformed from a reliable but run-of-the-mill sales guy to a bona fide partner—someone who was there not to hawk a new product but to get to the heart of their goals and help make them happen.

The Big Question:
How do your customers see you?

By any traditional measurement, Todd and his team had no soul-searching to do when it came to this account. They'd been doing reliable business for years, winning deals and bringing in substantial sums. They knew everything they needed to know about the account to show up at the right moment and get the deal signed. There were no external signs that anything needed to change.

But in shifting his perspective to consider things from the customer's point of view, a world of new insights opened up. After nearly a decade of knowing precisely how he saw his customer, Todd knew for the first time how his customer saw *him*.

What he discovered was that, while he had their trust and much of their business, the customer fundamentally considered Todd to be a transactional figure in their lives. He was there to make a sale and close a deal. He often arrived at their door bearing solutions they wanted or needed, but neither he nor his team was part of a bigger-picture play-book. Todd's team might have always known *what* the customer was doing, but no one mistook them for knowing *why* they were doing it.

It was when Todd took a step back and started to listen that he began to see the relationship potential that had been hiding in plain sight.

By understanding the *why* behind the *what,* Todd unlocked *two* critical advantages:

---

1. With a clear view of big-picture objectives, Todd could elevate himself from a guy with a bag of tools to a trusted advisor with a valued voice in strategic conversations. As a partner, you can earn the kind of relationships that open new, bigger, and more varied discussions—and with them, new, bigger, and more varied deals.

---

2. A firm grasp of the customer's priorities made it infinitely easier to direct where his own team focused. By knowing what mattered to your customer, you know what needs to matter for your own team. This kind of insight means less wasted energy internally and more value for the customer externally.

Todd's successes didn't go unnoticed. Along with the achievements of the other pilot accounts, it was clear that this new approach, which GE Healthcare dubbed outcome-based selling, had hit on something big. The results were so significant that executives codified the approach and access to the sales technology through a new selling program they named Ascend. They built a team of coaches, leaders, and others, to bring it to the rest of the organization. Todd was tapped to join the team full-time.

What the Ascend program brought to the organization wasn't a rigid methodology—in fact, Todd says teams regularly borrow bits and pieces from various approaches—as much as a new mindset.

"In the past, our sales approach could be boiled down to three steps: here's why you need my technology, here's how to justify it, and now I'll find a way to fit it into your problem." Today, that's been flipped on its head. "Now it's completely different. Now we say: 'What's wrong with what you're doing today? Why change? Why now? And over the course of the next six to 12 months, here's why you should partner with me to help solve that problem.'"

Old Approach	New Approach
"Here's why you need what I'm selling."	"What's wrong with what you're doing today?"
"Here's how to justify purchasing my product."	"Why change? Why now?"
"Here's how I'll fit what I'm selling into your problem."	"Let's work together to solve your problem over the short- and long-term."

In the years since the Ascend program's inception, Todd and his colleagues have carefully measured the data to track how the 70-plus accounts managed under account planning principles fare against the rest of the accounts within the business that are run with a more traditional approach. Ascend accounts reliably outperform, averaging 9% yearly growth as compared with 5-6% from the accounts managed more traditionally.

Revenue Growth % (YoY)

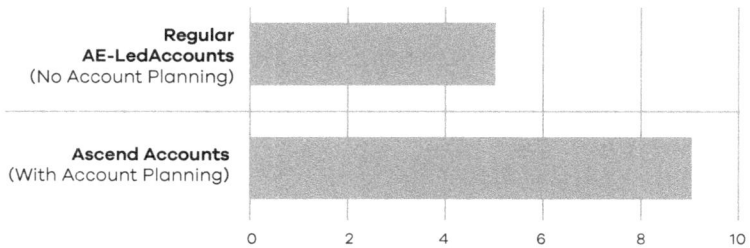

To this day, Todd thinks back to a conversation he once had with the CEO of a major healthcare system. "How do you get back into my office?" the executive had asked, "Just two things. One: you have to understand my business as well as I do, if not better. Two: you have to help me get where I need to go."

Todd says he knows it sounds simple. "But if it were easy, everyone would do it."

Three Lessons from Todd Adair

1. **You have blindspots. It's up to you whether they're uncovered**

   Challenge yourself: Do you know the answers to "why" questions, or only to "what" questions? Todd realized he knew plenty of facts about his account, but little about the vision that drove them. He needed to dig deeper with his account, which meant having conversations that weren't directly related to opportunities. He had to know what they prioritized in order to know how to position what he had to offer and become a real partner.

2. **Being vulnerable is worth the discomfort**

   Admit what you don't know and be open with your customers about how you're trying to deepen your understanding. Leaders called Todd out for not having asked the right questions in years past, but the exchange opened the door to a dramatically improved relationship. By exposing his own knowledge gaps in the context of a renewed commitment to filling them, he earned trust and respect.

3. **Better knowledge breeds better deals**

   You'll win more when you put your customer ahead of your product. Todd's new approach opened deal opportunities in places his company had never done business before and helped him better prioritize and coordinate the efforts of his team.

"It's not just about focusing on the opportunities of the deals, it's about focusing on a bigger agenda to help our customers deliver to their customers in the right way."

Jason Cooper
Head of Sales Excellence,
Johnson Controls

2

The End of the Lone Wolf Era

Jason Cooper is the Head of Sales Excellence at Johnson Controls, a global building technologies company with revenues of ~$25B. He has held positions in sales, sales management, and, for the last five-plus years, sales leadership, working across enterprise sales teams in the UK & Ireland to transform their sales environment for growth.

Jason Cooper was stumped.

The customer responsible for his head-scratching—let's call them ABC Construction—had been a source of internal consternation for a while now. Jason's company, Johnson Controls, had been doing business with ABC for more than 25 years. But as far as Jason, Head of Sales Excellence, could see, there was no reason that the two shouldn't be doing *more together*. ABC was one of the country's largest construction firms and their activities spanned all of Johnson Controls' key sectors. The pair was a natural fit.

And yet.

Quarter after quarter, sales numbers within the account fell short of expectations. Loss rates stayed stubbornly high.

Where were they going wrong?

Lack of tenacity certainly wasn't to blame. Sellers bid ABC

often. And it wasn't that the company couldn't offer value. They were often called in to support the configure, price, quote (CPQ) process, helping ABC close their own deals.

Nor could anyone argue that sellers at Johnson Controls didn't know their stuff. The company's extensive, technical, and highly complex products had spawned an equally extensive, technical, and complex sales organization. Every rep specialized in a particular building technology solution and prided themselves on their deep expertise. The Fire and Security team knew all there was to know about fire detection and complex security systems. The HVAC team knew heating, ventilation, and air conditioning inside and out.

The mismatch between effort, expertise, and actual results didn't add up.

Luckily, Jason isn't the type of leader to let questions go unanswered. "I'm a life learner," he says. "I've always got my nose in a book, a webinar, or a course to figure out how we can do things differently." He had a hunch that this was precisely the type of situation that called for some of that innovative thinking.

His team began gathering internal insights into how the company engaged contractors, how it was positioned, and how it could grow.

At nearly the exact same time, ABC got in touch. And what they said blew the lid off of Jason's search for answers.

ABC, it transpired, was frustrated. They didn't have a problem with Johnson Controls' products; the solutions ABC purchased from the company were top-notch. Nor were they peeved by the sellers themselves; the people they bought from were some of the most knowledgeable in the business.

What was driving buyers at ABC up the wall was the chaos. Sales reps, they griped, were coming at them from all angles. Everywhere they turned, it seemed, another seller popped up. "Sellers had an unstructured entry point to the customer," says Jason. "They were all coming in saying, 'I'm the one you should be speaking with!'"

Though all the reps were eager to talk to people at ABC, they were apparently less interested in talking to one another. No one seemed to know anything about other conversations that had previously taken place, or have a handle on who else was already engaged with the account. The results were unending confusion, a whole lot of noise...and one frustrated customer.

The complaint brought to light a disquieting truth: the company's individual sellers might be high-performing, supremely knowledgeable experts—but they were also driving everybody crazy.

Until that point, sellers had always engaged with ABC around specific projects, sending the fire suppression expert to one part of the business and the building management guy to another. It had made sense, at least in theory, given the complexity and specificity of each solution. "But the left hand didn't know what the right hand was doing," explains Jason.

In an attempt to structure sales processes in a way that allowed reps to exist within their own, individual spheres of expertise, sellers had found themselves isolated in silos, lacking the insight—and the incentive—to understand what was happening beyond the walls of their particular solution set.

But what to do about it?

It was clear that the company's approach to selling needed an update if it hoped to meet the expectations of customers like ABC. It was less clear exactly what that new approach would look like.

Jason and his colleagues put their heads together. Asking their sellers to trade in their expertise for shallow, far-reaching knowledge clearly wasn't the answer. Sales channels—and the expertise that resided within them—were one of the company's greatest strengths. And frontline sellers would always be the lifeblood of sales success. It was in sending them off on their own, however, that things seemed to fall apart.

It was time to tear down their preconceived notions and rebuild their selling strategy from the ground up. To do so, they'd need to ask themselves a series of important questions:

- Where are we now?
- What don't we know?
- Who can make the biggest impact?

Where are we now?

The first priority centered around data. Jason knew that this was no time for guesswork. He and his colleagues met with sales directors representing the full spectrum of internal sales channels and began to build a comprehensive picture of the organization's strengths and weaknesses.

They also knew that they'd need to think big. Silos had gotten them into this mess, and thinking within their bounds certainly wasn't going to get them out. The only real solution would need to be universal. So they reached up the ladder, securing the backing and buy-in of general managers and senior leaders who sat above the siloed structure. With these on board, Jason's team could be confident that, when change did come, it would reach across the sales organization as a whole.

What don't we know?

But the most important stakeholder was the customer itself. Jason asked around to figure out which seller had the best relationships within the account. She received a special assignment: "We told her, it's up to you to help us understand what the customer wants, and what their other, bigger-picture needs might be."

The rep took the assignment on with gusto. She opted for a direct approach, mining insights from everyone within Johnson Controls who had them to offer and then validating them with ABC. She proved not only willing to bring up their frustrations but also unafraid to probe further to learn everything she possibly could.

Her findings proved to be a gold mine.

"We unearthed a whole raft of different things," says Jason. The insights were extensive, ranging from how ABC liked to do business to their major priorities and how a partner could fit into their vision. But the biggest insight proved to be neither about specs nor projects: it was about values.

ABC Construction, they discovered, was deeply committed to sustainability. So, as it happens, is Johnson Controls.

"We worked out pretty quickly that our values really do align. We were both trying to achieve the same thing in our space," says Jason. "That was a game changer."

Who can make the biggest impact?

Armed with this critical insight, Jason set out to design a sales team that reflected the needs of ABC—not the internal divisions of Johnson Controls. Doing so would require people from across far-flung regions of the business to come together and share the fruits of their individual conversations. "We brought in sustainability experts and digital specialists to have different discussions with the customer so we could layer up our collective understanding," he says. Many heads, after all, are better than one.

How can we build trust and change perceptions—internally *and* externally?

But not everyone was convinced by the new philosophy.

Some sellers considered the idea of giving up valuable information about their accounts to be nothing short of absurd. After all, each sales channel, made up as it was of knowledgeable sellers, saw its fair share of individual successes. Would letting others into their processes risk personal quotas or put existing opportunities in jeopardy?

Reps asking these questions weren't out of line. They were simply reflexively protective over their positions in the account and of the contacts they'd worked hard to cultivate. The lone wolf approach, so deeply ingrained in many of them, had led them to think of themselves as solo actors who had the most to gain by operating alone. *Their* deals were *their* deals. There was no larger "us."

Jason and his colleagues realized that their new approach would only work if sellers stopped thinking in terms of "my deals" and started thinking bigger about "Johnson Controls' account." That shift, they knew, wasn't going to come easy.

It fell to Jason and his team to help the sellers see beyond their individualistic worldviews. Their unique skills and knowledge were valuable, but there were limits to what each rep could do on their own. To do so, he had to redesign the way sellers interacted with one another. He created a "closed environment" for account planning discussions around the ABC account. Jason told his reps, "We can't be having side-bar discussions outside of the account planning discussion." Everything had to happen within the group.

More than sales strategies or plans, Jason focused on building trust. One of the problems, he realized, was that his teams spent too much time on video calls and not enough time in the same, real-life room. "We weren't spending enough time together to really understand everyone's posi-tion, to be honest with one another, and to start address-ing the core issues," he remembers. "Relationships are diffi-cult to form virtually. From the first in-person meeting, time spent together facilitated a new direction." The very first get-together was so impactful that the team agreed as a col-lective that they had to get together physically at least twice per year.

Jason built on that momentum.

"When we're together, you should feel entirely safe being transparent," he told his sellers.

He paid particular attention to those who were reluctant to share the kind of information they were accustomed to keeping to themselves. "We encouraged everyone to outline their objectives and challenges around an account. When people got talking, they could identify with challenges and naturally started to spot the ways they could align as a team."

These exercises helped would-be detractors begin to change their tune. "Getting a peek at the bigger picture and hearing insights from across the team highlighted how nar-row their focus was," says Jason. "They couldn't help but start to see the value in the process."

As they spent more time together, a culture began to emerge in which people weren't afraid to tell the whole truth.

"We got to a place where sellers felt comfortable talking openly about success and failures," he says. "We talked candidly about our relationships with the customer and what we were hearing from them about what they wanted." The more they talked, the more natural it started to feel.

As trust grew, the conversations got more and more productive.

Reps who had previously been holdouts suddenly found themselves getting access and introductions within their accounts that they'd never had before, all thanks to their fellow colleagues. "Widening their network was a real breakthrough to change their beliefs," says Jason.

Over the next six months, the group aligned their insights about ABC's goals. Working on their own, each person could have the kind of in-depth conversations they were so adept at having within their particular areas of expertise. Together, they could bring and exchange their various insights so that the group could build a comprehensive map of ABC's vision—and figure out how Johnson Controls could help them reach it.

The investment was well worth it. When Johnson Controls sellers sold individually and operated within their product-based silos, ABC accounted for a pipeline of about $12 million and spent roughly $1.5 million annually. Two years later, when an account team spanning the business worked together to share insights and help each other sell, that pipeline had expanded to nearly $100 million, with an annual spend of close to $20 million.

"If we had stayed siloed, we'd still be where we were," Jason says. "The customer would still be frustrated, and we wouldn't have unlocked these opportunities."

The Big Question:
Do your sellers see themselves as lone wolves or as key players within a team?

Many reps view sales as a solo sport: *their* quota, *their* deals, *their* account. This mindset can make collaboration feel at best like a waste of time. At worst, working as a group can feel like a direct threat to everything they've worked to build.

In Jason's case, there was a good deal to be said for going it alone: internal silos and technically specialized product knowledge gave sellers very little reason to interact naturally. But when the team started to consider things from the customer's point of view, it became clear that sending reps out on solo missions was hurting *everyone's* performance in the account.

It was good, of course, that reps could bring such in-depth knowledge to sales conversations, but their hyper-focused channel selling model had created an unintended consequence: a disjointed approach that left the customer feeling perpetually pelted with disconnected proposals rather than being supported by a reliable partner.

Shifting away from an ingrained lone wolf mindset is a process. It took more than scheduling standing meetings or forcing reps to enter information in a shared database in order for Jason to get people to stop thinking as lone wolves and start thinking as a team.

The missing ingredient was trust. Trust in one another, yes, but also trust that collaboration wouldn't mean sacrificing their own goals to prop up someone else's sales numbers. Jason needed to help people see that everyone would win more if they pooled their information and built a better understanding of how to position themselves as a company.

Did it work? The numbers don't lie.

The Power of Mindset Shift

	Before: *"It's my account and it is my job to make sales."*	After: *"It's Johnson Controls' account and it is my job to help them achieve their goals."*
Pipeline	$12M	$100M
Closed-Won	$1.5M	$20M
Win Rate %	2.4	5

By taking the time to build trust internally and share information, Jason's team gained access to a crucial insight (the customer's shared commitment to sustainability) that opened the door to an entirely new, significantly more strategic, account-based approach. Then, by putting together a coalition of experts who could deliver on these values, the company elevated itself from a vendor to an essential, trusted advisor.

It's worth noting that change was as gradual externally as it was internally. "It doesn't happen on day one," says Jason. "It took about two years to move into the role of a trusted advisor. It took time for our account managers to really work with the team. It took time to make the right introductions and build the right relationships. And frankly, behaviors needed to change on *both sides*. Both we and ABC needed to rethink how we worked together. They had historically treated us like a transactional vendor. We both needed to make adjustments if we were serious about realizing our ambitions."

Today, Jason's reps have conversations they never had before. "We're invited now to go and sit with their teams—

and almost be a *part* of their teams. It's a really interesting change from just selling opportunities for single solutions to being a true partner in this space."

Word of what Jason's been up to has spread. "One of the biggest indicators of success for me is people want to be on this account. They're circling around and seeing some of the results. When people are knocking on the door asking, 'How can I be a part of this? What are you doing over here?' That's success. And it's not only our sales managers and heads of sales—it's our leadership team that wants to be a part of these sorts of planning sessions."

The reason people have taken notice isn't because of the numbers (though they certainly don't hurt), but because his approach has moved beyond the lone wolf era and into a future of strategic teams who are stronger together than the sum of their parts.

"It fundamentally changes your culture if you get it right," says Jason. "It really does."

Three Lessons from Jason Cooper

1. **Lone wolf sellers achieve less than those working in a pack**
   Some sellers will be reluctant to embrace transparency and share information for fear that it will hurt their own numbers. In fact, collaboration opens up the kinds of big-picture insights that cement long-term relationships and grow pipeline for everyone. Insights, introductions, and ideas grow exponentially when sellers are able to work as a group.

2. **Internal alignment begets external alignment**

    By combining both the insights and the efforts of a diverse group of internal stakeholders, you can approach your customer with both deep knowledge about their goals and the skills and resources to help them get there.

3. **Teamwork requires trust**

    Collaboration doesn't blossom overnight. You'll need to build a safe environment in which sellers can see the value of transparency and let go of a zero-sum mindset.

"It isn't just about deals. It's about figuring out how we can create an incredible customer experience."

Scott Jackson
Senior Director, Sales Enablement,
Comcast Business

3

Win, Retain, Grow

Scott Jackson is a Senior Director of Sales Enablement at Comcast Business, Enterprise Solutions, where he helps sales teams develop the skills they need to win complex deals in blue chip accounts. He has over 20 years of experience in sales and marketing and has served in the U.S. Army — first as a soldier, later as an Airborne Ranger Infantry Officer.

When you speak with Scott Jackson, it's not surprising to learn that he began his career as a member of the United States Army. He has the kind of gruff, clear-sightedness that makes you sit up and pay attention; a presence that suggests you'd do well to assume that anything he chooses to say will be worth hearing. These days, he's taken his talents to his career's third act, as a sales coach.

It hasn't always been an easy job. But spending his days guiding people invigorates Scott. He sees it as his mission not only to help salespeople through their day-to-day lives but also to broaden their thinking beyond transactional contracts and quotas to the realm of account planning.

"It's my goal to help sellers see that it isn't just about deals. It's about figuring out how we can create an incredible customer experience," he says. "How can we help *our* customers create unique business value for *their* customers?"

It's not always a mindset that comes naturally.

"When you come up in a sales culture that doesn't think strategically nor does account planning, everything is opportunistically focused," Scott says. "A lot of the salespeople I encounter basically just show up in front of potential customers and say, 'Here's my list of tools; what can I sell you today?' instead of coming in with the intent to understand more deeply how they can help someone achieve their goals."

Scott continues: "It's a challenge for people to begin reframing their approach of understanding who's who within an account and what value we want to create for them. It really is a paradigm shift."

But Scott believes it's a shift worth making.

When he can successfully encourage his sellers and their colleagues across the business to take a wider, more customer-centric approach, big things begin to happen in every area of sales, from retaining existing footholds against would-be usurpers to expanding within existing accounts and even winning new customers altogether.

In this chapter, we'll take a closer look at the ways account planning has helped Scott's reps win, retain, and grow their business.

What does it take to retain your position?

One of Scott's sellers had held an account for 10+ years. Rather than take it for granted over the years, he had made it a priority to establish himself as a trusted presence. He'd taken the time to get to know the right people within the business and always made space to listen to their plans, goals, and concerns.

At every step, he made sure that his customer knew that they were heard and understood and that Comcast was aligned internally to help solve their problems.

But one day, bad news arrived: The customer wasn't renewing. They had decided they needed a different product mix—one they could only get elsewhere.

The two sides parted ways.

That, it seemed, was that. Until the rep got a call 16 months later.

"We're midway through our implementation with our new vendor," said the voice at the other end of the phone line. "But it's just not working for us. We know you didn't have exactly what we were looking for, but when we were with you, we always knew that you would be there to help solve our problems."

The rep nodded along. But what, exactly, were they saying?

The customer took a breath. Then: "We've decided to come back."

The rep was shocked. The contract had been dead and gone, lost over a specific set of needs. Yet here the customer was, like a long-lost love at the end of a romantic comedy who shows up with a bouquet of roses and the admission that the breakup had been a terrible, terrible mistake.

And, like a romantic comedy, it was happily ever after.

"We were so well connected across the organization," says Scott, "all the way from the seller up to our CFO. Everyone had relationships they were responsible for, not only just to cover, but also to evolve, mature, nurture and advance. That was a big part of why they came back—we knew their business and they were well covered before they walked away."

This is not a traditional story of simply playing defense, and it's all the more compelling as a result. Scott's customer left because of product details—and ultimately returned in spite of them. Even when it may have appeared that all hope was lost and that there was simply no way to win against a competitor who had the exact technical capacities the customer was looking for, Scott's team still prevailed. They had invested in showing up when it mattered, and that investment came back to them in a big way.

"This was probably our biggest win-back deal ever," says Scott. "We earned more than we were making in the previous contract across all 21,000 sites."

Ultimately, their customer decided that partnership was even more important than product. Regardless of specs, they knew that in returning to Comcast, they'd have access to a group of people working together to further their goals. And that proved to be the most valuable product capability of all.

Where can you expand your footprint?

Comcast held a contract with a grocery chain that operated 3,000 stores across the country. The contract was a good one, but Scott believed there was room to grow. He got his team together to figure out how.

First, Scott focused on the people. "I'm always asking: 'How can we get higher and wider within this organization?'" he says.

There were the usual discussions, of course, about who they knew and how healthy key relationships were. But Scott also encouraged his team to think beyond traditional business ties and consider how they might be linked within their real-life communities.

"Even after 10 years, I'm always shocked about how often there end up being local connections," says Scott. "But it always happens: one contact's kid is on a soccer team with a kid of one of our employees—there's always some sort of connection we can tap into to help us get to know people on a deeper level."

Here, Scott's team benefited from a special program they have in place called "Exec Connect."

"Exec Connect helped us leverage all of our executive relationships that are local—execs who are on the same board, who live in the same area, or who are connections on LinkedIn. It's thanks to this program that we found and built the kind of local executive connections that would ultimately make all the difference."

Second, he honed in on understanding the business pressures that were driving decision-making and prioritization for the customer. "I don't want you to just find out about their business requirements," Scott told his sellers. "I want you to figure out how they seek to differentiate from their competitors in the marketplace."

Members of the team set out to do just that. They asked good questions and, more importantly, listened to what key people within the organization had to say.

Over the course of their conversations, they reached an important conclusion: The chain aspired to present itself within its communities as a local brand.

Now, Scott told his reps, it was time to tap into the knowledge Comcast already had of the customer's industry.

"Let's bring them the business insights we have from working in this industry and proactively tell them about what we're seeing other grocers doing and how we can help this company create similar value," he told them. "What kinds of solutions are these other companies using that we can now sell to this brand, knowing their big-picture goals?"

With these questions in mind, it was time for the team to map the opportunities before them.

They started by pulling a list of all the solutions similar customers were using. How many of these did this customer already have? How many were they missing?

"We call that the solution landscape—others call it whitespace analysis, but the same ideas apply," Scott says. "We're simply trying to match what's working and use that as a jumping-off point to expand. Once we know what they're missing, we orient to help them see why doing more business with us and buying these products will help them accomplish their big goals and create the competitive differentiation they're after."

How can you drive new business?

Scott's team set its sights on acquiring a net-new contract with a large dental business. It had more than 3,000 franchises around the United States, each one representing between one and 10 sites.

"When choosing an opportunity, there are a few things you need to consider," says Scott. "The types of questions we ask are: 'Where can we make the biggest impact to effect change? Will the location enable us to make a big splash? Is it somewhere we can make a difference while also showing our project management expertise?'"

While the account met the profile, it also came with its fair share of challenges. For one, the company was privately held, meaning minimal information was available to the public for Scott's reps to consume, understand, and work into their sales strategy.

The second was the business model. "When you think about franchising, it's a very decentralized approach to decision-making," says Scott. "That made it even harder for us to easily scale and make a single, compelling argument about how we could solve their customer experience problems."

The third was, if anything, the trickiest: the goods Scott's team were selling simply weren't top of mind for the potential buyers. "Their experience and their focus are in doing the work of dentistry," explains Scott. "They're thinking about people's mouths, not about their Wi-Fi connectivity or secure transactions."

To help focus his sellers, he repeated his guiding questions to them like a mantra: "Why change? Why now? Why Comcast?"

Striding into thousands of dental offices with Power-Points about internet speeds clearly wasn't the way to go. Instead, Scott steered his sellers in another direction.

"To begin building those relationships, your starting point is to listen," he told them. "We have limited information and expertise about their business. We need to hear them and figure out how we can make a difference."

His rep set out. He spent time talking to people with influence and insight to get a concrete understanding of what mattered to them. Over time, he earned their trust.

Why change?

Over the course of his conversations, the rep began to see that his real competitor was the preexisting mindset. Initially, the franchise owners simply told him they'd prefer to stick to what they had—usually a local provider—because it just didn't seem like there was any compelling reason to make a switch. "All I need is Wi-Fi for my office," they'd tell him.

Scott wasn't surprised to hear this. "More often than not, the biggest competitor I have isn't another vendor. It's what I like to call 'Do Nothing Incorporated,'" he says with a chuckle. "It's always easier for a buyer to give in to their fear of failure and default to saying 'No'."

Why now?

"What we need to do," Scott told the rep, "is to help anchor the value creation on the customer experience, not the nuts and bolts. In their current mindset, they aren't considering the possibility that we can do more than just connect them to the internet."

In building relationships with key people within the account, Scott's rep had earned the right to start having deeper conversations about how the two businesses could work together.

Why Comcast?

Comcast, he told them, could offer Wi-Fi, just like their existing providers. But it could also offer them secure connectivity for their work in the back office. Not to mention, the company could make it easy to put up TVs in the front lobby to keep clients entertained while they waited for their appointments.

Because he had built up a strong reputation, the rep was able to inspire his contacts to think bigger and, ultimately, to act.

"It wasn't a big-splash event," says Scott. "We had to get 300 decision makers to come in and make this choice, but we won a large site and then built up momentum as we moved across the country."

By keeping customer goals fully at the forefront of their minds, Scott's team was able to come into the new account, unseat the competition, and win at scale.

The Big Question:
How can you use account planning to improve your standing in every sales scenario?

The ethos of account planning runs deep. It's not a set of tricks to get you in the door or speed up a deal—it's a fundamental reorientation of your company around your customer. It's this focus on the big picture (i.e., your customers' success) that makes it so supremely versatile.

Regardless of whether you're striking out into a new account, growing within an existing one, or simply boxing out the competition, account planning keeps you focused on the activities that help you drive mutual value, and more revenue to your bottom line.

Win

Discussion around account planning often takes place in the world of existing customers, but it can play an equally substantial role in winning new business. The same principles that organize a team around understanding and serving a current customer will also help you to stand out from the competition when wooing a potential new account.

Existing relationships form a platform

With roots deeply spread across your customer's key influencers, you'll have an inside track from the start. Your head start in the business of trust can help you shape buying requirements before would-be competitors even know there's a deal to be won.

Relationships with the right people

Prioritizing finding people with influence within an account will help you earn support and avoid being blindsided by an unknown detractor. (We'll talk much more about this in Chapter 10.)

Deep customer knowledge

Buyers are used to being approached by brazen sellers who know everything about their own products and nothing about the customer they're trying to acquire. Account planning pushes teams to do their research and prioritize learning above all else. By showing up with questions and insights instead of product-centric answers, you'll set the tone for trust-building from the start.

Alignment with customer's top priorities

By taking the time to listen and understand what your customer's biggest goals are, you'll be able to ensure the services you provide deliver consistent value and open the door to future opportunities. Understanding your customer's pain points will also enable you to provide solutions to problems that are not apparent at first glance.

Retain

Retaining your position within an account can be as valuable as any other sales objective. Keeping your spot not only means renewal of a hard-won deal; it also means not ceding territory to a rival, as well as setting yourself up for expansion down the road.

Account planning makes retaining your relationship with a customer possible by making you and your company indispensable in their success in a few key ways:

Accessing a team's-worth of knowledge

As we will see in Chapter 12, aligning internal teams around account priorities means sellers are in direct and regular contact with people who have different viewpoints on an account. Customer success managers, for instance, may have deep and important knowledge about areas of growth for the customer that may offer opportunities for you to broaden your partnership. By working as a group, you ensure these crucial insights aren't lost in translation.

Consistent value through internal collaboration

By bringing people across your business together to work with the account, you can avoid random, uncoordinated contact and instead make sure that everyone, from your CSMs to your renewal managers, contributes to a single, high-value relationship. If and when the account changes hands, newcomers can quickly get up-to-speed with centralized information. When you don't allow cracks to form, nothing can fall through internally—and no one can break in from the outside.

Trust

By focusing on customer priorities, providing value, and creating a wide set of relationships with the people who matter throughout your customer's organization, you'll have the crucial buy-in from people who competitors might approach. When key players know they can trust and depend on you, it's much more difficult for a new and shiny option to turn their heads.

Account planning makes you a rock. Retaining revenue in accounts depends on deep insights, far-reaching relationships, and strong internal alignment. Account planning allows you to rally your team around your customer and leave no room for an outsider to unseat you. Your competition doesn't know what you know, can't align the way you align, and hasn't earned the trust of the people who matter.

Grow

In addition to fostering loyal customers, account planning also opens avenues for expansion within an account by giving you a clear view of where you can create the most mutual value.

Insight into growth opportunities

Understanding your customer's business priorities and earning a seat as an advisor at the strategy table is an inside track to future opportunities. It's also a much better vantage point from which to see where your customer's business is going. When the goals of the business overlap with the unique value you can provide – boom! There's your next opportunity.

A vision for achieving customer goals

Rather than thinking about a singular deal, teams consider how they might be able to help a new customer successfully pursue *their* priorities. Thinking one step beyond signing the contract helps your potential customer see that you're committed to their success, not just to making the sale.

Taking what you learn into the next opportunity

Gaining access to the customer's strategy table, and showing what great looks like within their industry, grants you knowledge about the best practice, solutions trends and other insights that can help similar customers move the needle.

Bringing the business insights gained in this way, while staying focused on the big picture, helps you proactively demonstrate value and expand into new customer accounts.

Three Lessons from Scott Jackson

1. **Building great relationships is worth the effort**

   When the company in Scott's first story left for technical reasons, it would have been tempting to think that the work of relationship-building had been a waste of time. But when they began to have second thoughts about their new vendor, the ties of trust Scott's rep had created made it easy for them to make the choice to return.

   Above all else, customers want someone who can solve their problems. The specific capabilities of your products matter, but not as much as a product-centric seller might be prone to believe.

---

2. **Show up with something to offer**

   A true partner is someone who helps you advance your goals. Scott saw this when his team pursued an expansion with a grocery store chain. One value he knew his team could bring to the table was their knowledge of the industry, and he used those insights to help the customer see that Comcast was ready not only to provide the tools they needed but also the knowledge that could help them make the biggest possible impact.

Expansion is easiest to sell when it supports a compelling vision. When you can see clearly how your offerings overlap with your customer's goals, you can make a case that feels both natural and urgent.

---

3. **Delivering value starts with understanding your customer**
   Scott's sellers didn't just barge into the dental offices with a list of technical specs. They took the time to listen and understand the needs of the offices and consider the ways that they might be able to do more than just turn on a Wi-Fi router. It was thanks to understanding their customer's business that they were able to solve problems that weren't at first apparent. When they made the pitch, Scott's reps highlighted the way their work would help the dental franchises make *their* customers' experiences better and solve additional business challenges that went beyond the immediate solution.

   Gaining a deep understanding of your customer allows you to see where products fit in the larger narrative that is motivating your buyers. When you arrive with a story that centers your *customer's* customers, the product you're selling plays the part of the supporting cast rather than stealing the show.

Part II

Conquering the Pitfalls

"I'm never going to use this."

Travis Hill
Managing Director, Strategic Consulting,
Upland Altify

4

A Visit to the Graveyard of Good Intentions

Travis Hill is the Managing Director of Strategic Consulting at Upland Altify. With over two decades of sales experience, he's led multi-year, multi-million dollar sales transformation initiatives with some of the world's largest sales organizations. He's managed five of Altify's largest accounts, including three within the Fortune 15.

Phil Trapani is Principal Consultant at Upland Altify. A sales process expert, he has been helping sales leaders operationalize account-based selling best practices for 12 years.

If you're serious about introducing account planning in your organization, you certainly don't want to end up in the crowd of executives insisting to one another: *"It seemed like a good idea at the time."* The truth is, *knowing* that your organization will benefit from account planning is only the first step. An important first step, to be sure, but a first step all the same.

It's in bringing the practice to life that you'll show your real skill as a sales leader.

That's why this chapter, perhaps paradoxically, is about sales transformations gone wrong. The subject may seem dreary, but I think you'll agree that it's a whole lot better to read about failure than it is to experience it firsthand.

Sales leaders with big dreams for improving their organizations are a dime a dozen. Those who actually shepherd said dreams from idea to reality are a rarer breed. I've seen up close the attempts of many sales leaders to steer their teams toward a grand vision of success. Some realize their goals, while others watch in horror as their efforts fall flat.

Why?

Change is hard in the best of circumstances, and sales leaders face thornier challenges than most. Sales is fast-moving and personal. Everyone, from the most junior sales development rep to the most experienced director, harbors entrenched belief systems, relationships, and ways of working. Straying from the predefined path could spell lost deals and lost earnings, which makes any adjustment at once an opportunity and a risk.

The very best salespeople are always learning, growing, and experimenting, but the rest generally prefer to stick with what they know.

But we need everyone. Account planning, as we've already seen, is a team sport.

Bringing best practices to an entire organization is a tricky business, and charging forward without a plan can spell disaster.

In that spirit, we'll use these next few pages to take a look at two true stories—one about the implementation of sales methodology and one about the implementation of sales technology—to shine a light on the many pitfalls that trip up even the most well-meaning efforts to boost sales performance.

Like explorers adding to a map, the missteps of those who've gone before us help chart the storms and sea monsters threatening to thwart our expedition. By studying the route and making the proper preparations, we're far more likely to see danger coming and steer our ship into calmer waters before it's too late.

In my experience, there are a handful of key requirements for success. Lose any of these, and you're bound to veer off course:

- Simplicity
- Belief and trust from your sellers
- Effective and recurring enablement
- Tools and methods that meet the needs of the full team.

As you read each story, keep an eye out for what's dooming the attempt. In the second part of the chapter, we'll map out exactly where things went south.

Story #1

Two years, hours of training, and one departing sales leader later, there was simply no denying it: the attempt to adopt a new sales methodology had failed. Travis Hill almost wished he was more surprised. But like many of his fellow sales reps, he'd seen this coming from a mile away.

It had all started when Travis got his job at the software company. After receiving his logins and his company-branded t-shirt, he'd also been given an assignment: to enroll in an internal, months-long methodology training course.

Travis was no stranger to sales training. In fact, in his very first job out of college, he had found himself in a nine-month intensive program during which he had been handed a stack of books on topics ranging from negotiation to neuro-linguistic programming and told to start reading. On the first day of training, there had been 90 sellers. By the end of his six-month contract, just two remained. "I went through the wringer," he remembers.

But his hard work had paid off. Within a year and a half, he had been entrusted to oversee a team of sales development reps. In six more months, he had been asked to launch an entirely new program. Over the next two years, he had taken a business unit that generated zero revenue and turned it into one that pulled in $40 million per year.

Learning wasn't something a guy like Travis was going to shy away from.

But as far as the material went, this was a first. While the intensive sales boot camp he'd gone through in his first job had focused on what made a good seller, this class was more narrowly tailored to a specific—and, he'd soon learn, quite complicated—methodology.

A (confusing) mandate from above

The methodology in question had been mandated from on-high. The sales leader was a believer and knew that a successful organization needed its sellers to be on the same page. So for a full afternoon every week for nearly a year, Travis found himself herded into a classroom after lunch for four hours of instructor-led learning. The approach he and his fellow sellers were being trained on didn't seem like the best fit for the product, but the sales leader loved the system, and that was that.

To Travis, though, the practices he was learning seemed excessively complex for the kind of work the company did. "It wasn't difficult to understand," he explains. "But it was difficult to put into practice, particularly because it didn't necessarily fit with the kind of style that some people on the team had."

He wasn't the only one who felt unconvinced. When the clock struck five and they were dismissed, reps would get together to chat. Mostly, though, they just laughed. "I'm *never* going to use this," they'd chortle, leafing through their stacks of handouts and notes.

And for the most part, they were right.

As far as Travis could see, the extensive classroom course was the start and end of the methodology's relevance to his life. No one in company leadership tracked adoption. No one told reps how they were expected to put what they'd learned into practice.

"No behavior change expectations were communicated," says Travis. Nor did anyone make an effort to tie the methodology to success. "The idea of driving better win rates was what was discussed when we were learning," says Travis. "But as far as I know, they were never able to measure whether there'd been any impact."

Without anyone reinforcing what sellers had been taught or proving that it would make them better at their jobs, most people went back to business as usual. "We very rarely stuck to the methodology unless there was a big deal that we knew was going to be under extra scrutiny from leadership," Travis remembers.

The result was what Travis dubs "circumstantial adoption." When reps were asked to do something in adherence to the methodology, they did. Otherwise? "They probably wasted a lot of money on that trainer, because no one was doing anything unless they were asked to."

And they were hardly ever asked to. Travis's manager seemed largely uninterested in how he was selling, as long as he was hitting his numbers. Nor did his manager seem motivated to offer meaningful guidance of any kind. "My manager never got into relationship strategy. He never asked what problem we were trying to solve for the customer or how we were planning to get it done," remembers Travis. "All he asked was, '*When is this gonna close? How quickly can you close and for how much?*' We never got into any real deal coaching."

Without being required to use the methodology, reps were more than happy to forget all about it. The times they did need to use it, the steps felt like chores rather than useful strategies. Instead of making their lives easier, the motions they'd been trained in seemed hopelessly cumbersome. "It felt like it was way too much," says Travis. "It was hard to justify spending the amount of time that it required."

Two years later, when the sales leader left the company, the methodology—and the hundreds of hours worth of weekly afternoon training sessions—left with them.

"It stopped entirely," Travis says. "Nobody taught it. Nobody used it."

Story #2

When a company asked Phil Trapani for consulting help, they were exhausted. For two years, they'd been trying to roll out account planning to their organization with the help of a technology platform. When Phil arrived, they had absolutely nothing to show for it. For all the time and money they'd invested, the tech was sitting idle, used by almost no one.

The company was a large one, with more than 40 sales leaders and a track record of success. But they knew they could do more—and grow more—within their existing accounts if they moved sellers from a "me" mindset to an "us" approach.

To earn growth with their customers, leadership knew, teams would have to consistently deliver measurable value. But coordinating the seven or eight people working with each account—from customer success, account managers, and account executives to solution sellers, product marketers, and professional services—they'd need to find a way to bring together the siloed, ineffective, outdated, and duplicate information circulating about the customer so they could deliver real outcomes.

They needed to overhaul their digital collaboration. They needed software.

After a hearty amount of comparison shopping and due diligence, the company selected a vendor and began implementing the new platform.

It wasn't long before there were early signs of success. Top sellers were creating plans within the platform and delivering big wins.

But all that glittered wasn't gold.

"You can write an account plan in any technology," explains Phil. "The success looked promising, but really, it was just the best sellers moving what they used to do in PowerPoint into the new platform."

For everyone else, success wasn't coming quite so naturally.

The platform they'd installed was supposed to help sellers stick to the new account planning best practices. It would, the idea went, create continuity and consistency by guiding sellers through an approved way of working. But in reality, it was proving to be a little too instructional.

Theirs was a large company, with a host of teams that looked different, worked differently, and had different objectives. "Partnership teams that are selling through channels or selling through value-add resellers—their account plans aren't going to look the same as enterprise teams or small, medium business teams," explains Phil. "Most companies typically have three, four, five different selling motions. Large complex organizations can have as many as ten to 15."

But the software didn't reflect these variations. Instead, it was rigid, designed to work only to guide sellers through one particular motion. And one size, it soon became clear, did *not* fit all.

Every manager needed to be able to speak the same language in order to collaborate and share information, but they also needed to be able to guide their teams in ways particularly suited to their skills, personalities, and objectives. Again and again, they found, the tool just couldn't adapt.

What's more, the tech asked a lot of its users. The over-complicated application was intended to help sellers adopt best practices, but instead, it gave people the added work of having to follow a complex set of rules that didn't always make sense for the things they were trying to achieve.

"It became too heavy; it was too hard to use," says Phil.

Instead of taking something off of sellers' plates, the technology had heaped on extra portions.

After two years of using the technology, the company had little to show for its efforts, save for a few disgruntled sales reps.

Quietly, platform usage rates slowed to a trickle, then dried up entirely. And with them, for the time being, went hope for widespread adoption of account planning.

What went wrong?

Oof. Those two stories were hard to read. Especially because both stories featured leadership teams who started off with the best intentions. In story #1, the leader recognized the importance of a common approach to selling. In story #2, the company understood that digital collaboration and tech-enabled processes are essential for successful account planning.

But in each case, it didn't take long for good instincts to break down into wasted time and effort. And the longer each organization spun its wheels, the faster people abandoned ship.

Let's break down some of the major shortcomings:

Mistake 1: Too much complexity

Even after they'd finished sitting through hours of sales training, Travis and his fellow sellers chafed at the sheer amount of busy work the methodology required them to do. "You'd literally have to go to the printer and print things to fill out in order to use the methodology," remembers Travis with a shake of his head.

To make matters worse, the extra effort didn't seem to serve any particular purpose. The methods seemed out of touch with his actual work. "I didn't agree with the amount of complexity in the methodology and how to apply that to the deals that I was pursuing or to the accounts that I was managing," Travis says.

Advanced methodologies have their place in modern sales, but trying to stretch them to cover all teams and all products can often unnecessarily complicate sellers' lives. (Account planning, for the record, is simply a set of best practices that can work alongside any methodology and scale a common language between them.)

Phil, too, witnessed an excess of complexity. The technology the company implemented asked too much of its users, often in ways that didn't make sense. At times, the tech was so opaque that users didn't know what terms even meant. And when people don't understand something, they aren't always going to do what it takes to figure it out. "People aren't going to pick up the phone and call someone to ask, '*What did you mean by this?*' They're just going to move on," explains Phil.

Technology is essential for account planning, but overly complicated systems will do more harm than good. A platform is only useful if it's easy to use.

In each case, the complexity came at the expense of the adoption of new behaviors. And with so much asked of sellers, it didn't take long before people abandoned the system altogether. Travis's training classmates tossed aside their worksheets and printouts in favor of their own methods, and sellers at the company Phil encountered soon decided that attempting to manipulate the sales technology to do what they needed wasn't worth the effort.

Mistake 2: Top-down orders without universal buy-In
Travis learned the methodology in the classroom, but then rarely heard it mentioned again. His manager didn't require him to use it, nor was he coached in how to apply what he'd learned in training to the real-life deals in front of him.

And his own bosses shared his distrust. He explains: "It's almost always the sales manager who says, '*I don't want my people to spend this amount of time on something that isn't useful.*' And so that's where it usually falls apart."

Without buy-in from the full organization, usage of the methodology was restricted to instances in which reps knew higher-ups were watching. Even though executives believed in the system, no one on the ground had been consulted or convinced, and no technology had been introduced to keep people accountable or on track. "Frontline sellers trying to close deals are going to revert really quickly back to what they know," says Travis.

The real fragility of the adoption became clear when any mention of the approach vanished the moment the sales leader who championed it was out the door.

Mistake 3: Additive work

In both stories, we got an up-close look at what happens when sales strategies ask more of their practitioners than they offer in return.

Travis needed to follow a set of cumbersome steps to comply with the demands of the methodology, which rarely helped him work the deal. Phil's customer's sellers had to figure out how to use complicated software that couldn't meet their individual needs. "You couldn't adapt," he says. "There was only one way to use it."

In both cases, sales teams ended up with extra work instead of tools and best practices that could help them get more done.

Mistake 4: Focus on the few, not the many

In our second story, early successes with the platform seemed like clear proof of the technology's promise. But Phil argues that great salespeople can recreate their existing success with any platform. "Sure, they had some great progress in pockets of their sales team," says Phil. "But I'm sure that people who followed account planning best practices did so because they always have. The thing is, they would have been just as successful in PowerPoint—and that wasn't the problem anyone was trying to solve."

Real gains take place within the majority of sellers, not the eagles who will thrive anywhere. "If you can make your average-level sellers 5% better, *that's* where you'll make a massive difference," argues Travis.

Mistake 5: Tech without methodology; methodology without tech

Tech and methodology need one another. In big companies, large numbers of people must be able to work together, share information, and communicate their insights and progress in a common language that is accessible to all.

In Travis's experience, strategies taught in a classroom fell apart without their presence in his day-to-day life. Without being prompted by integrated tech to proceed in a specific way, he and others reverted back to old techniques. When Phil arrived at his customer, he witnessed technology that wasn't equipped to guide sellers in ways that made sense for their area of the business. In both cases, sellers were missing a crucial piece of the puzzle.

"Science helps us improve every aspect of modern life, and complex selling is no different," says Phil. "A good selling platform without science—or the wrong science—is just a piece of technology. But when you blend the right science with the right technology, you'll make the experience better for both buyers and sellers."

Best practices taught in seminars or saved in personal folders will soon wither. And tech that doesn't reflect a seller's specific approaches or the team's common language won't get used. Only when these two reinforce one another will you derive real value from either.

How can we avoid this mess?

If there's one thing you should take away from these cautionary tales, it's the truth that a good idea is just the start. Account planning has transformative potential, and realizing it requires a clear vision, full buy-in, and the right tools.

If so much can go wrong, how can sales leaders move forward with confidence? What do you need to put in place to ensure that bringing account planning to your team doesn't end in wasted time, wasted effort, and money flushed down the toilet?

If the road to hell is paved with good intentions, the road to the account planning promised land is best trekked with the right map, the right gear, and the right people at your side.

In the next chapters, we'll get to ride along with leaders who've charted the path to success. You'll see exactly which foundational pieces are essential to an account planning framework that's built to last.

"Getting people on board required two things: the carrot and the ego."

Eric Chapman
Vice President of Sales Operations and Enablement,
Hexagon Asset Lifecycle Intelligence

5

Introducing Account Planning (Without Losing Your Mind)

Eric Chapman is the Vice President of Sales Operations and Enablement at Hexagon Asset Lifecycle Intelligence, where he's overseen 11 quarters of continuous growth nearing $500m in annual revenue. He previously held director positions in sales strategy at Hewlett-Packard.

Enough with the doom and gloom. You've earned yourself a happier ending.

If the last chapter was all about the ways leaders can veer off course, this one is a portrait of what things look like when change-makers stay on track.

For it, we spoke with Eric Chapman, a sales veteran who has seen the industry from nearly every angle.

"I started my career at the bottom," Eric says. "I was an order admin processing contracts." Not for long: "I just kept moving up." For more than 20 years, Eric proved himself and advanced, rising through the ranks of Hewett-Packard before earning his right to a string of major strategic positions.

Though his roles differed over the years, his interest only crystallized. "No matter where I was, I kept gravitating back to the same goal: I wanted to optimize the processes that would help sales," he says. "Every time I got into a project, that's where I found myself going back to."

He was good at it, too. Soon, he found himself running sales operations, compensation, sales strategy, and growth initiatives and tackling the inefficiencies of CRM systems.

His success prompted a call from Hexagon, a fast-growing software company that needed somebody to run its brand-new sales operations and enablement function for its PPM division globally. The challenge, should he choose to accept it, was to build this new sales muscle from scratch. The moment was critical. As the company expanded, the foundations it put in place across its sales org could spell the difference between smooth sailing and shipwreck.

Was he up for it? Eric said, "Yes."

When he arrived, he found that his starting at square one had not been an exaggeration. "Everything was brand-new," he recalls. "There was no sales methodology, and a lot of the foundational things were missing." For some, the situation would have seemed dire. For Eric, "It was a perfect opportunity."

It was time to get to work.

What makes methodology?

Encountering a sales team without a formal sales methodology was a new concept for Eric. Over his long career, he'd worked under the prescriptions of more than his fair share of codified sales systems.

"I think every sales leader who comes in has a new method," says Eric. "And I've probably been through them all and tried to operationalize every one."

Which methodology would PPM's CRO introduce? Was having a traditional methodology even necessary for success?

Or would it simply end up as a clunky distraction in the form of a theory? Eric got thinking about the approaches he'd learned and implemented over the years. What had worked? What hadn't? What could he take away from his experience?

Then it dawned on him.

"All the methodologies share a basic underlying element," he says. "It's simply how you can organize what you're doing to grow your business."

What had really made a difference in his career, he realized, hadn't been whether he'd be using one methodology or another. It had been something more subtle. "The most important thing I ever did was to switch from an internal organizational view to seeing everything through the lens of the customer. Where is the buyer on their journey with us? What does the buyer need as an outcome? What do they value? All of these things are so much more important than specific internal metrics."

The true value of methodology, he realized, was primarily that it served to organize the sales team. It equipped them with a centralized and consistent set of definitions to describe the things they were trying to accomplish and allowed everyone to work out of the same playbook fostered by a system that was easy for the sellers to leverage.

When it came to what would make the difference for Hexagon's customers, Eric set his sights beyond closing more deals. Instead, he focused his energy on how his new sales team could work together to do just that. "Everybody sells," he says. "And the selling team needs to work as a team to achieve the customer's desired outcomes."

Putting account planning in place would allow him to rally everyone who interacted with the customer across the organization around a common language and set of processes without clouding the ultimate goal: serving the customer.

Where can we make the biggest gains?

It was tempting to kick things off with the best sellers his new company had to offer. After all, it was they who won the biggest deals and made the most significant individual impacts on the business. It seemed logical to prioritize whatever could be done to help these high flyers soar even higher.

But Eric resisted the urge. Instead of making the best people better, he turned his sights on the rest of the sales org.

The decision was based on a simple observation: "Great sellers are usually great without any system in place," says Eric. He knew that optimizing the processes of people who were already at the height of their game might offer him a higher floor, but it also capped him with a shorter ceiling.

If top salespeople were like individual skyscrapers already towering above the city, atop which he could add another floor or two, the "B and C players" were the vast swath of mid-rises that, with a little retrofitting, could transform the skyline.

With his target in mind, Eric began to think through the ways he could introduce sales processes and technology that could lift average performers from transactional deal makers to the builders of mutually beneficial relationships. "I knew that account planning could help them have better interactions with customers and, more importantly, not stumble into avoidable missteps that might lose them deals." Rather than trying to overhaul everything they did, Eric looked more carefully at the behaviors that left money—and customer outcomes—on the table.

"Some aspects of selling are intangible or are beholden to variables we can't control," he says. "But I knew that if I could elevate their game with coaching and systems that allowed them to reach a point at which the customer trusted them and felt heard, I'd know that I'd helped them achieve something they wouldn't have on their own."

This, he decided, was his #1 goal.

What needs to change?

To make the gains he envisioned real, Eric would need to change the way his average performers worked. They were already comfortable singing the praises of Hexagon's products, but now they'd need to build the kind of trust, knowledge, and relationships that would allow them to have meaningful conversations about their customers' goals. If they could make the shift, they'd free themselves from their transactional mindsets naturally. "If sellers are thinking about how the customer will benefit, they can't be thinking just about closing the deal and hitting a quota," Eric explains.

Many of the B- and C-level sellers, though, were comfortable with where they were. They didn't always exceed their quotas, but many reliably hit 90% or even 100%. To motivate them to think bigger, he'd have to get them to see that focusing on their customer's goals wasn't a purely altruistic endeavor. Rather, that it "turns into sales, sales, and more sales."

The key, he knew, would be to get sellers out of their small-scale mindsets—single deals closed by individual sellers—and encourage them to think more holistically. "It's not about a specific seller getting the win independently. It's about how we're collectively solving the customer's business problems. We need the team to say, '*We own this plan.*'"

Moving from "me" to "we" would require a change to relationships *internally,* not just externally. "Sellers have to feel comfortable pulling in anyone, from other sellers or pre-sales services to contract ops, renewal management, and others who have their own insights into a given account. And they need to see that as an opportunity to work together rather than a scary moment in which they're inviting outsiders to barge in, inspect their plan, and criticize it."

Account plans did already exist at Hexagon to an extent, but they were almost exclusively relegated to large accounts and housed in manual PowerPoint documents. To scale the approach, Eric needed to take the idea to the rest of the organization.

He knew that a significant proportion of the company's revenue was tied to existing accounts, which meant that add-ons and upgrades were normal goals for most of the sales team. What *wasn't* normal was a more ambitious understanding of growth. Eric wanted his sellers to see that meaningful expansion wasn't going to come from piecemeal upgrades: it would come instead from adding new offices and buying locations within existing customers and expanding into new prospects in new industries where the sellers didn't have the long-standing relationships.

To help sellers reach these new streams of income, he'd need to make it easy for sellers to see their whitespace and work together to develop strategies that would expand Hexagon's reach.

How can we convince people to change their behavior?

Introducing account planning was one thing, but getting it to stick was another.

Senior leadership understood the need for change (they'd hired him, after all), and were quickly convinced that thinking bigger via account planning was the best way to do it.

Reps, too, were often willing, at least up to a point, to start tackling plans for a few of their larger accounts. "Most actually already had some level of a plan in their head," says Eric. And though they may have thought it was enough, "in reality they were maybe 60%, 70% of the way there." Rather than tell them they weren't at 100%, Eric opted to show them. "As they started to document it with account planning in an actual technology platform, they quickly spotted gaps and were prompted to think through considerations that wouldn't have occurred to them otherwise." Getting the information down, they quickly realized, wasn't just admin work: it was active thinking.

Frontline sales managers were less convinced. As far as they could see, trying to keep a handle on their sellers' myriad plans would be no small task.

"Getting managers on board required two things," says Eric. "The carrot and the ego."

The carrot was to be found in the organizational hierarchy. "Leadership made it clear to frontline managers that account planning was not a suggestion—it was an expectation," says Eric.

The ego was a more delicate matter, one that required an element of psychology. He considered what might encourage supervisors to adopt the new approach. Did they need to be named and shamed? No, that wasn't right.

Then, a lightbulb went off: "Sales managers love to be winners."

If he could turn early adopters into mini-celebrities, people might perk up and listen.

So he went looking for managers who had embraced account planning and, subsequently (though not surprisingly) had begun to see success. Then, he invited them on stage.

At sales kickoffs and in audiences with the leadership team, the chosen few were ushered into the spotlight. "They told the story themselves," says Eric. "And having them show off how they were using the account planning processes to lift their teams' performance was so much more effective than anything else we could have done."

There, in front of their peers and superiors, early adopters got their time to shine. And laggards saw what they were letting slip through their fingers.

How can we prove value?

Eric was well aware that the early days of a new sales process were always precarious. He needed to make sure that sellers at all levels saw account planning as a permanent approach, not the pet project of yet another self-important sales leader.

Above all, account planning would stick once people saw that it worked.

But there was no universal definition of what that looked like. For each practitioner, Eric would need to tease out a different set of evidence to prove value.

With more transactional sellers, he focused on making a connection between disparate efforts. "What seems to resonate is that the outcomes the customer is trying to achieve are borne out across multiple sellers selling different components of our portfolio," he explains. "When these sellers take a holistic approach instead of focusing on their particular product, everybody achieves more."

Mid-enterprise sellers, too, started to see the way account planning could be relevant to them. "They might be selling a lot of relatively small deals against a quota, and each one can feel transactional if they're seen in isolation," Eric says. "But when they map out their plan and see that they're short of their goal and don't know how they'll make up the difference, they recognize that they might be able to get more out of these so-called transactional opportunities. It might change how they prioritize their efforts."

Getting volume sellers to invest in account planning was particularly tricky. "Turnover is higher," Eric explains. "Sellers may be there for only one or two years. They're not thinking long-term, which means mapping a long-term strategy for a customer's objectives is far less appealing than just zooming in on this year's quota—*maybe* next year's."

For this group, he shifted tactics to help them see the value closer to home. "Train your brain now," he told them. "Because if we see you creating great plans, that's a strong selling point for a promotion into enterprise selling. And you better believe that when you get six or seven enterprise accounts, you're going to need to be able to do this."

Though the tactics— territory plans vs. account plans— were different, the results were the same. Again and again, Eric found that those who gave account planning a serious effort never looked back. "People who have picked it up haven't stopped using it," he says. "We don't even have to keep reinforcing it after a little while."

As adoption took hold, the conversations Eric had with sellers began to change. During the first year, he'd been fielding questions like, *"Why am I doing a plan?"* Midway through the second year, however, reps began to see that the up-front work they'd done mapping their plans hadn't gone to waste. "It's a living document from one year to the next," says Eric. "And they started to look back and see how much they'd accomplished, as well as how the insights and new relationships they'd developed were now making a big difference."

When accounts changed hands, new sellers had detailed records of what the customer needed and what had been done. Before, sellers had complained both about having to come in cold to an existing account *and* about contributing to a plan for the sake of future owners. Now, the value was clear.

Taking a wider view also helped sellers think ahead. "Some reps are terrible at thinking about their future pipeline until the set of deals they're currently working on is done. If we can get them thinking about that next set now, they can start some of those calls earlier, speed up the velocity of those deals, and not fall into a cycle in which they have spikes of wins followed by long lulls of inactivity."

How can we create lasting change?

The only way to get people to see value, of course, was to ensure that they actually invested in account planning long enough to generate results.

One thing was clear: he couldn't do it alone.

To keep people at it, Eric had to make sure that the entire sales organization lived and breathed account planning.

During the early stages of the account planning rollout, Eric's team asked managers to track the details: how frequently were plans being updated—or even opened? Over time, however, he was able to start taking a more holistic view of how sellers were using their plans in the first place.

One major venue for introspection was sales KPI reviews. During these meetings, sales leadership and managers gathered to inspect how teams were progressing toward their quotas. Eric trained people to see all of the typical questions through an account planning lens. "If we see that a team is off track and isn't using account planning, that's going to open up a discussion," says Eric. "And it's not just with the rep—it's with the sales management team, all the way up the chain. We'll ask them to speak to where they are against their plan, and if it's silence, we know there's a problem."

When it's clear that the team is using account planning, the conversation unfolds very differently. "If they're rattling off information about their customers and how they're working toward common goals, the conversation changes to leadership asking, 'Where do you need help? How can we help your customers get through the challenges you've highlighted?'"

Now *that's* a conversation worth having.

Talking about account plans has been key to reinforcing the discipline. "If it's not part of reps' conversations with their managers and leaders, it's going to get shelved. If you're looking at it every month, on the other hand, you'll avoid a big surprise at the end of the year."

Tangible results, says Eric, are also the best way to make account planning last, no matter who's in charge. "As leadership changes in an organization, it's critical to be able to demonstrate and recap success and evidence of account planning's impact. It can take a very short time for new leaders to change course or pull attention away from account planning, so keeping them bought-in can save your organization from taking a few steps backward."

The Big Question:
How can you chart a course to successful change?

Like many sales leaders before him, Eric arrived at his new company with a mandate and a dream.

As the company grew quickly, getting the sales processes right would be critical. An expanding number of sellers needed a framework to collaborate, orchestrate handoffs, and of course, deliver the kind of real results to their customer base that would earn them the right to do more business.

Throughout his own career, Eric had seen leaders come and go, many brandishing bold new ideas that ultimately fell by the wayside. The success of *his* sales operations push would depend on his ability to introduce a framework that...

- ☑ Everyone could understand
- ☑ Everyone could use effectively
- ☑ Made a demonstrable difference for sellers and their customers.

Account planning was the way forward, but bringing it to life would test his abilities as a sales leader.

How'd he pull it off?

Smart Move 1: Keep the universal simple

Rather than forcing a complicated methodology into places and onto teams with which it wouldn't fit, Eric opted for a broader set of account planning best practices that organized people around a common framework and allowed them to stay focused on the ultimate goal: advancing the needs of their customers.

"Our modern conception of 'methodology' arose in the '70s and '80s when a handful of star salespeople decided to try to bottle up what they did and sell it," says Travis Hill of Upland Altify. "But really, a methodology is just a series of best practice sales behaviors. It's that simple."

Account planning's straightforward yet transformative goal—to build long-term relationships that create mutual value for a company and its customers—provides enough of a framework to organize sales efforts at scale without getting bogged down in details or stepping on the toes of existing, more complicated methodological approaches already in place locally within a sales org.

"Especially in big organizations, you need guardrails for internal communication," says Travis. "You need a set of generic business language, because if you end up with a bunch of terminology that you have to look up to understand, it's never going to get used."

This overarching language should serve to unite, not control.

"Most of the organizations that I've worked with have had multiple methodologies going on at the same time, but none that could scale across everyone, and that's usually the problem. That's where the language comes in: there are certain behaviors that you want to reinforce, regardless of the sales motion."

So long as the broader sales organization retains simple, universal standards that allow them to work together and report on their success, teams are free to design their own, more specialized approaches that make sense for their needs.

Smart Move 2: Focus on potential over star power
While leaders in Chapter 4 got distracted by false positives

from elite sellers (remember the eagles closing big deals in a new software platform with plans they could have designed in PowerPoint?), Eric turned his attention to the rest of the sales organization.

"If you think of your standard distribution curve, 60% of sellers are your B and C performers," says Travis. Shifting that curve 5% to the right makes a massive difference across a large sales organization."

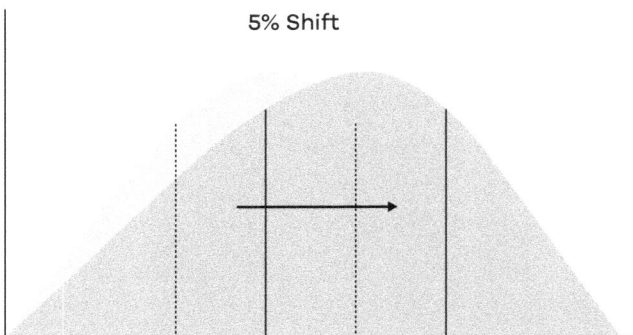

5% Shift

Smart Move 3: Reinforce consistently

In our disaster stories, perhaps the biggest problem of all arose from lack of follow-through. New systems were introduced by leaders far removed from the day-to-day realities of sellers' lives, and these practices tended to wind up ignored unless someone high-ranking showed up to check on things.

Eric, on the other hand, ensured that account planning became part of the very fabric of the sales organization. He put it on stage to showcase success at the manager level and made account plan reviews the first and last stop of every important sales meeting, from manager-rep check-ins to high-level KPI meetings with leadership. Account planning became the standard, and it changed the conversations people had about their work.

Eventually, the results will (and did, for Eric) speak for themselves. But as the transformation takes hold, it's critical to reinforce expectations in every area of the business to ensure that teams go through the proper motions and build a foundation for long-term success. Account planning takes time to unveil its full impact, but sellers can only reach that stage of maturity if they're guided, encouraged, and held accountable along the way.

Smart Move 4: Unite method with tech

In the campaign for behavior change, technology is a crucial ally.

"As a sales leader myself, I can honestly say I have undervalued the benefit of in-product guidance in the past," admits Altify consultant Phil Trapani. "Shame on me." Beyond leaders and managers, account planning software reenforces the right behaviors at every step of the sales process so that nothing is left to chance.

Technology can also help leaders see what's working. Visualization is a leader's best friend. No matter how organized your record-keeping is, it's impossible to know where you stand until you can see it laid out in front of you. "You can't chart progress if you don't have consistent use of methods, and when it's laid out in technology, now you have the data you need," explains Phil.

Smart Move 5: Get everyone all-in

Reinforcement at every turn isn't possible without buy-in across the sales organization, from leaders to managers to disparate departments and teams.

Eric made sure he had champions at every level of the organization who would help make account planning real. Instead of issuing edicts from on high and hoping the reps would follow through, he shored up the support of leadership and management and made account reviews an integral part of sales culture so no one could confuse it for a pet project of a single executive.

This factor is so critical, in fact, that it deserves its own chapter.

Shall we?

> "*Account planning is about driving the biggest possible ROI from the activity of your sellers.*"

Eddie Pyrtle
Sales Excellence: Value Selling Coach,
Qlik Technologies

6

Going All-In

__Eddie Pyrtle__ is a sales coach helping organizations strategize, develop, and execute operational programs that drive sales effectiveness and efficiency.

Eddie Pyrtle was there to listen, not to talk. He'd just joined a new company as a sales leader and coach, and his first priority was simply to get the lay of the land. Far from a lack of ambition, Eddie's initial inaction was carefully designed to allow him to maximize his understanding of his new landscape—and his ability to transform it.

"For the first 30 days, I was just a sponge. I was listening with the goal of assessing and understanding the sales organization's current state," he says.

At the end of the month, he was invited to join account plan reviews. The team gathered in the conference room and began to discuss the accounts in question. For his part, Eddie was "just a fly on the wall, trying to figure out what we were doing in the accounts." For the next hour, he watched, brow furrowing more and more deeply, as sellers described the basics of their accounts, recent activities, and short-term opportunities.

"After a while, I realized this wasn't really an account planning exercise. It was a profiling exercise at best. It seemed very reactionary. There wasn't a lot of strategy. There was no path forward. Nobody knew who owned what."

With increasing effort, he kept his mouth shut, even as his mind raced.

After the meeting was over and the participants had left the room, Eddie found himself alone with the sales leader. He held his opinions in, waiting to hear what the leader thought about the meeting. He braced for the leader to smile and tell him that the account reviews had gone exactly as he had hoped.

Instead, the leader turned to Eddie, his face looking pained. "Man," he said with a heavy sigh. "Can you tell me what the hell just happened?"

That question, as Eddie remembers it, was "music to my ears."

Music? Why was the sales leader's consternation such a welcome tune? Where the sales leader saw a mess, Eddie saw only opportunity. "That comment from the sales leader was a really good signal that this was the right time to implement an account planning discipline. Everywhere you looked, there was low-hanging fruit."

But how, exactly, would he go after it? Before Eddie lay two paths.

The first was the road of minor change. He could introduce a small pilot program, perhaps engaging the company's star sellers as test subjects. He could hold a few workshops on sales best practices and make some upgrades to the tech stack. It was, at least at first glance, the safer option.

The second was a thornier route, with a steeper incline leading off into the unknown. It would involve introducing sweeping changes not only to the sales team but to the organization as a whole. Should he choose to traverse this path, success in this direction would require more effort on his part, as well as the collaboration and cooperation of leaders across the business.

Or at least, those *would* have been the two paths available if Eddie were the type of person who ever considered giving anything less than 100%. As far as he was concerned, there was only one route that could take the team where it needed to go.

Eddie attributes his sales success—and the professional philosophy it inspired—perhaps ironically, to his non-selling background.

"Like many sellers, I started my career in a non-sales yet customer-centric industry role," he says. "This mindset has been invaluable. I've never lost sight of what it means to be a customer, and this has changed the way I present myself and my product. It's how I help create and execute strategy for the organization; it's how I lead and coach sales teams. Always, the customer's perspective is front and center at all times."

It was clear that account planning, with its primary focus firmly on rallying people around customer success and business outcomes, could fix the disorganization Eddie had witnessed.

"Account planning is really about aligning activities and resources to execute against big-picture strategies. It's proactive, not reactive. It's about revenue and retention, of course, but fundamentally it's about driving the biggest possible ROI from the activity of your sellers."

It was evident that, as it stood, the sales team wasn't maximizing its own value. By upgrading the way sellers worked—and the way they worked together—he knew he could change that.

He also knew it wasn't going to be a minor undertaking.

Change starts with buy-in

Money was tight. Without access to unlimited funds, it was crucial that Eddie make his investment both intentional and worthwhile.

To get the implementation he envisioned, Eddie would need to win consensus. He met with leaders across the organization, from marketing to customer success and beyond. "There are a lot of people who need to be on board with account planning to make it work, not just sales," he says. "Because their people are going to be members of the extended account teams that work together to serve the customer. I had to make sure I had the commitment and buy-in from cross-functional leaders. Otherwise, we'd have been doomed from the start."

Earning success required him to make a compelling argument to his colleagues. Each of them, after all, had their own goals and visions for the future of their teams, and wouldn't be swayed away from them without a good reason.

"It was important that my colleagues outside of sales had an understanding of why they were critical in the process," says Eddie. "It was my job to explain the expectations of how they'd contribute to the account team and how the success of the wider team would help drive success with our customers. Many of them immediately saw that participating could be a real career-development opportunity for themselves and their team members."

When he'd gotten the buy-in he needed, he made his way to the CEO. They spoke in detail about what they would spend money on, and, just as importantly, what they wouldn't. "I thought we were ready to sign and go," remembers Eddie. But the CEO held up a hand. "Guys, I get it," he said. "We're all on the same page. We agree this is something we need to do. But a lot of organizations make decisions to do something, then invest and roll out and make the change. But they don't necessarily get the bang for their buck." Everyone nodded. It was a story that felt all too familiar.

"I want you to come back to me," he continued. "And bring me a very detailed change management plan that you'll use to help ensure we maximize the investments we're going to make."

Eddie took the directive to heart. "I knew I needed to keep it very simple so that everyone could internalize and understand what we were doing," he says. "So my approach was centered around clear milestones."

At every step of the journey, from communication to roll-out and beyond, "I always thought ahead to ask myself, 'How are we going to measure this?'"

He broke the process down into *three* key phases.

---

1. **Deployment**

   "Before going live, I went back to stakeholders and reminded them again what we'd talked about to make sure nothing had changed," says Eddie. Only when he was confident that everyone was fully on board would he begin enabling the sales organization with the new sales technologies and methods.

---

2. **Enablement**

   "We can't just tell people what we want them to do and send them off to do it," explains Eddie. "This isn't a check box to tick and move on from." After the initial roll-out, he planned follow-ups complete with best practices, user guides, and support. "Sales leaders are a really big part of this. We designed playbooks with the goal of making it really easy for them."

---

3. **Reinforcement**

"Once you get to that adoption phase, it's time to really get into the operationalizing process," says Eddie. He told his team to be on the lookout for success stories and opportunities to share best practices to keep account planning—and its impact—top-of-mind for everyone. And he committed to making himself available for coaching, "whether at the leadership level, team level or one-on-one." He knew that it would be time well spent. "If you don't keep it top-of-mind, other things can slip in and get in the way."

At every phase, he considered the reporting and analysis he'd need to use to track what was working and which areas needed additional support, all with the goal of maximizing investment. "Tactically we measured account plans and reviews completed, account team follow-up cadences, new customer success stories, and internal account planning success stories," he says.

He also kept key performance metrics top-of-mind, including:

- Annual recurring revenue (ARR)
- Net promoter score (NPS)
- Customer satisfaction
- Revenue growth
- Pipeline growth.

How do we use sales leaders as allies to reinforce account planning?

At every step, Eddie made sure he wasn't acting alone. "Executive sponsorship is key. Communication is important, but it makes far more of an impact if it comes from the right person." Eddie found creative ways to make sure sellers got the message, including using videos of the head of sales that featured personal messages reminding watchers of why they were doing account planning and why it mattered for the company, the customer, and the individual reps themselves.

At the team level, he engaged sales managers lower down the chain to work with higher-ups to lead kickoff events that reinforced the belief that adopting account planning would be a productive use of everybody's time. "It's nearly impossible to have success without both the executive sponsor and the sales team leader being bought-in and offering support."

Since the account planning gospel was being preached by their own management, not just far-off sales leaders, reps heard a message that hit closer to home. In every meeting and presentation, Eddie made sure his messengers reinforced the relevance of account planning. They focused on overall corporate goals and strategies, as well as specific current go-to-market initiatives. Only once reps internalized these ideas did he move on to coaching and execution.

How do we overcome resistance?

This commitment to deep understanding extended to dealing with the few remaining holdouts in the room. "There's always resistance," says Eddie. "Generally it's the minority, and usually, there's a reason behind it."

Rather than simply force them to change, Eddie made a point of understanding where the people pushing back were coming from. "Generally, people who resist have some sort of risk or exposure, real or imagined," he explains. "Maybe that individual's knowledge isn't as deep with a particular account as they may have led others to believe. Perhaps they don't feel that they have the necessary skill set, and there's fear associated with that. Or maybe they're just the type of person whose instinct is to keep information close to the vest and are reluctant to share."

In other cases, reluctance stemmed from sellers' unique insights. "I've seen several examples where the account owner knew from their own experience that it wasn't the right account to start with from a strategic, long-term perspective. Their resistance might simply be that another account within their territory would be a better fit."

Getting a handle on *where* the resistance was coming from was essential to understanding how best to overcome it. In some cases, Eddie even had to step in and make adjustments to make sure everyone was set up for success. "We realigned a few territories and certain accounts within territories because one account needed a more strategic, long-term focus. We didn't let reps go, but we sometimes pulled them from one account and put them with accounts they were better suited to lead."

Real change, Eddie knew, couldn't just come from the individual level. "Account executive sponsors and even the CEO should be reviewing strategic account plans because sales wants to know that the work they do matters and is meaningful. There's nothing more frustrating for a seller than to do this extra work, only to get questions from their superiors that make it clear they haven't taken the time to review or assess the plan."

"We've got to drink our own Kool-Aid at the leadership level. We've got to act interested and engaged. It's not enough to simply say, *'Go off and build this.'*"

How do we get people over the hump?

No matter how good the rollout was, Eddie knew that change never happened overnight. Nor could he expect adoption to progress in a straight line. "It's really a cycle," he says. "After the methodology and the technology were introduced, it was all about reinforcement and getting people to wrap their heads around what they were being asked to do. I had to strike a balance between keeping things simple and challenging people at the same time."

Some of the reps Eddie worked with "acted almost like it was a no-brainer." *I get it,* they thought. *Now get off my back.* "People thought it was no big deal until they got hands-on and started to really do it. Not until they had to actually go deeper and execute, did their attitudes change," Eddie says. "At this point, they struggled a little. And that's not a bad thing! Because it's at this point that they started to see the benefits and outcomes we'd told them about. Only then did it become real for them."

As sellers moved past the one-year mark, Eddie could tell that a shift was underway. "With the first account plan, folks were in learning mode. They were looking at this new methodology and tool and thinking, *'How do I even do this?'* But once they got to the second or third account plan, the lights turned on, and the *"aha!"* moments began."

How do we keep up the momentum?

As time went on, Eddie could tell that sellers increasingly knew the drill. They understood the expectations and had begun building account plants without nudging or hand-holding.

But movement and turnover are inevitabilities of the trade, and Eddie knew that he needed to design systems that could keep the momentum moving no matter who was on the team or how experienced they were. "It's always an ongoing effort," he says.

"We may have previously enabled people, but that doesn't mean I'm not going to do refreshers on an ongoing basis, especially in key areas of focus. Understanding the customer—their key business drivers and priorities, measures of success, growing key relationships, and creating S.M.A.R.T. goals—seems straightforward, but a lot of people struggle with it. So we keep showing up and reminding them how differentiating themselves in this way will help them be successful *and provide value* to their customer."

Eddie realized that he couldn't expect people to change their entire approach without support. He made additional internal sales coaches available to help people get better in any and all areas. Of key importance was creating a safe space for sellers. "Account owners and the extended team needed to know that they were safe to ask questions and get help in any way they needed. It could be refreshing on a concept or working with a sales coach who could help them think through aspects of an account or deal they hadn't fully considered." This openness and support helped keep people on track who may have otherwise thrown up their hands and given up.

How do we know that we're succeeding?

No matter how many internal success metrics you set, there's nothing so valuable as a good interaction with customers.

But how could he know for sure that his efforts were paying off?

One rep Eddie coached recognized the value of account planning right away. He zeroed in on his customer, getting to the heart of their key business drivers, their goals, and their strategies and going so far as to travel to meet with the customer's executive sponsor to validate his findings and ensure alignment, positioning himself to help as well as he possibly could. And with a big renewal on the horizon, the rep returned once more.

When the rep brought up the renewal, the executive paused. In the silence, he walked over to his desk and opened the drawer. Had the rep said something wrong? What was going on? The executive pulled out a stack of papers.

"Yes, I do want to talk to you about the renewal," he said. "But I'd also like to review with you again our company strategy this year and our approach moving forward. I think we should map out our route for the coming year and identify areas where we can work together. The renewal is important, I know, but there are other things we need to talk about, too."

It was at that moment that the rep realized that the papers in the stack were the company's key business drivers. He saw that they were a collection of their most important goals, strategies, and initiatives that had been developed to chart the course of the business over the next three to five years—and that these goals were the outcome of a strategy session the rep had facilitated some months prior.

Those papers—and the executive's eagerness to discuss them—were irrefutable evidence that the account team's efforts had paid off. Their hard work over countless account planning exercises and their commitment to validating priorities and collaborating with important players within the account had been anything but a waste of time. They had provided the kind of real value that helped to differentiate them from competitors and win long-term trust.

This was the proof Eddie was looking for that his efforts had transformed the sales team. "That single action by the customer is the greatest validation that you're doing account planning right. It's proof that you've moved from being just another vendor to being a true trusted advisor."

The Big Question:
How can you ensure account planning takes hold in your organization?

Deciding that account planning is the way forward can be done on your own. But bringing that vision to fruition calls for all hands on deck.

It requires going all-in.

Treating account planning like a side project you can dip a toe into is a recipe for disaster. Those who succeed in implementing account planning are those who secure buy-in, make a plan, and stay the course. Eddie succeeded by adhering to *four* important principles:

---

1. **Get everyone bought in**

   By definition, account planning is a team sport. It's the coming together of a whole host of people, from reps to presales, customer success managers, professional services, marketers, partners, and more who work together to pool insights and deliver results. The list of stakeholders must span across departments as well as reach from the top to the bottom of your organizational hierarchy.

And collaboration doesn't just mean giving a thumbs-up from afar. "True collaboration means active participation in account planning events, contributing to the details of the account plan, ongoing cooperation with the account team, and owning the execution of the plan," Eddie says.

Eddie started at the leadership level, involving executives from across departments and even getting the nod from the CEO. Before the rollout began, he even returned to each of them to confirm that he still had their full support and cooperation.

Getting backing is practical behind the scenes but is also important from an internal marketing perspective. Eddie deployed executives as company-wide ambassadors for the new program and also used team leaders to spread the message at a more local level to win hearts and minds.

When practitioners see that the strategy has the support of everyone from their team leader to their CEO, they'll see that account planning has staying power and will thus be much more likely to take it seriously and commit to changing behavior in the long run.

---

2. **Set goals ahead of time to measure success**

Every seller knows the importance of numbers, and implementing account planning is no exception. In the process of winning support from leadership, Eddie established milestones and metrics against which he could track his progress.

With clear expectations agreed upon in advance, you can earn the space you need to bring change to life, ensure momentum, and maintain internal investment and support.

---

3. **Teach, then teach again**

In Chapter 4's failure stories, we saw the way that even the most in-depth learning can evaporate if it isn't reinforced. Eddie built continuous learning into his long-term planning, repeating important lessons and making coaching available for anything reps might need help with.

"You can make all these investments into account planning methodology and tools, do a big rollout, do some follow-up, and think you're off and running," says Eddie. "But if you're not careful, some sellers might build some initial plans and then think they're done."

People never internalize everything, especially not in one go. Offering ongoing support, both in person and with coaching embedded in your account planning technology, is essential for reinforcing best practices and upgrading new behaviors from unfamiliar ideas into habits that stick.

---

4. **Know that it's a journey**

Impact from account planning isn't the result of flipping a switch.

"Account planning is a journey," says Eddie. "It's designed to help ensure ongoing alignment, not only with your customers but also internally. It's not about the short-term gratification of checking a box and chasing an existing opportunity. You'll have short-term successes, yes, but it's more important to stay focused on long-term gains. It's about ongoing validation, collaboration, and realignment, both with your team and with your customers."

Importantly, though, it's a journey that can be completed successfully by leaders who embrace the challenge. And because people like Eddie have blazed the trail, others now need only to follow the path that is proven to lead to real results.

The magic of account planning is in the big picture. It's the executive who invites you into the inner planning circle after a year of trust-building. It's a customer who abandons an entrenched vendor to go all-in with you after growing to see you as a trusted advisor. It's doors opened into new expansion deals you'd never before dreamed of chasing. It's a journey, sure. But the destination is well worth the trek.

"In our business, outcomes, not contracts, are our North Star."

Nigel Cullington
Upland Altify

7

The Key is Continuous

Account planning is the conscious rejection of old-school sales thinking. In years past, some salespeople had the unfortunate habit of treating sales like a hunt. Sellers were predators; buyers were their prey. To close a deal was to win the game. While that may still be true on the used car lot, in enterprise sales, this mentality doesn't get you very far.

In our business, outcomes, not contracts, are our North Star. When we navigate toward helping our customers win, our own wins will be right behind.

As we saw in Part I, this approach fundamentally transforms the ways seller and buyer interact. Teams that refocus their internal energy on considering the big picture of their customers' goals gradually begin to evolve the real currency of selling: relationships. We've already seen a host of examples of teams who, after months or even years of rallying internal stakeholders around their customers' success, found themselves earning a coveted invitation to the strategy table.

In other words, they went from being viewed as just another vendor—the kind who knocks on the door to sell a product—to earning the role of trusted advisor, one who can be relied upon when it counts most.

Over the course of this evolution, pipeline, opportunities, and revenue grew as a natural byproduct of the one thing that matters most: a solid relationship.

In Part II, we asked: "How are great account planning operations born?" To answer that question, we examined the stories of four organizations—two that succeeded, two that failed—to get a sense of what it takes to make the leap, and how we can learn from those who fell short.

In every story, we followed a leader who was up against significant odds. There were entrenched belief systems to upend, suspicious sales reps to convert, and wary customers from whom to earn trust.

Above all, these leaders were up against the ease of inaction. They had to overcome the siren song of sticking to the status quo. How much easier it must have seemed to each of them to invest less than 100%—to skip the technology or to overlook the average performers. How tempting it must have been to avoid the legwork of securing buy-in from fellow leaders across (and beyond) sales and the relentlessness of reinforcing best practices at every level of the organization. And yet the successful leaders met their unique challenges head-on.

Now it's time to ask the most important question of all.

How do you ensure account planning lives up to its potential?

The winners we covered resisted the path of least resistance because they understood one fundamental thing about account planning: It's continuous.

Account planning isn't an exercise you do once. It isn't something you set and forget.

Account planning is something you do every day. It's the catalyst for collaboration, the guidance for deal and account strategy, and the best practices that shape the opportunities sellers pursue, the people they speak with, and the goals they set.

In Part III, we'll take a detailed look at exactly how to bring continuous account planning to everything your teams do. We'll pull back the curtain and give you an up-close, in-depth look at the mechanics required to make your account planning engine hum.

We'll cover:

- **Building insights** that will help sellers join forces across teams to paint a comprehensive picture of your customers
- **Qualifying your way to success** by helping sellers develop an eagle eye for which deals and accounts deserve their attention
- **Knowing who matters** within an account so that reps can see beyond the org chart and uncover the critical structures of influence that define an organization
- **Support and scale with technology** by creating the conditions in which account planning can thrive
- **Running reviews** on deals and accounts that help your sellers make real progress by fostering productive, action-oriented discussions supported by diverse viewpoints.

If you're ready to reap the rewards of account planning and put it into play for your organization, these next pages are your proven playbook.

Ready?

Part III

The Playbook

"Hold your nerve."

Sarah Walker
Managing Director, Enterprise,
Cisco

8

Qualify Your Way to Better Sales

Sarah Walker is the Managing Director for Enterprise Business at Cisco in the United Kingdom. She previously held myriad senior leadership roles at BT Group, including Director of Corporate and Public Sector Business.

At the start of her career with BT Group (formerly known as British Telecom), Sarah Walker didn't think much about qualifying deals. No one she knew did.

And why would they?

"There was less competition then, less choice. So you didn't have to work quite so hard or think so creatively about how to win," remembers Sarah. "A lot of the time, you could get to the finish line on the brand name alone."

It meant that thinking critically about which deals to pursue wasn't part of her sales process. "We simply chased the deals that looked the easiest to win—the low-hanging fruit that would most quickly lead to cash."

But even as the deals rolled in, she began to wonder whether there might be a better way.

Sarah had been in sales since the beginning of her adult working life. "I found myself in sales completely by accident," she says. After finishing her A-levels and casting

around for a way to spend her summer, she landed a tempo-
rary contract with BT selling analog mobile phones. She so
impressed the company over the three months of her contract that they agreed to sponsor her university studies.

After university, she joined the sales team full-time.

In her early years, Sarah didn't receive any formal sales
training beyond the preferences of whoever happened to be
heading the department at the time. "In my formative years,
it was basically just learning on the job, knowing your products, and hoping that would be enough to succeed."

But Sarah gained enough experience to develop her own
guiding philosophy: "I saw that good selling starts with customer focus and curiosity," she says. "You have to have an
outside-in lens, always. Anyone who's focused on their own
products and their own business more than they are their
customers' is unlikely to do well."

Her instincts served her well. By leaning into her curiosity, Sarah started to discover things about her customers
that other sellers overlooked. She started to ask better questions and think more about the opportunities that landed
in front of her. Just three years post-graduation, she earned
herself a leadership role.

It was time to take stock of her new sales team.

Her reps were selling at a rapid clip, that was for sure. But
was it for the best?

"We had quite a lot of volume business coming through,
but we weren't doing anything particularly interesting or
creative with customers," she recalls. "I had a feeling that
we could do more."

Her solution? She wanted to focus sellers on what she
dubbed "transformative deals"—the kind of partnerships
that made a big difference for the business and their customers alike.

It wasn't an obvious move.

Prioritizing bigger, more impactful contracts would be a zero-sum game. It would require restraint. It would force sellers to think beyond simply meeting the requirements customers were looking for. It would mean that sellers would have to walk away from some deals in order to invest their efforts into others.

Would it be worth it? She decided to test that hypothesis.

Sarah reached out to the procurement officer at one of her biggest customers and asked for a meeting.

In the past, they'd had a fairly standard relationship. He'd let her know what he was looking for, she'd bid, and often, they'd sign the deal. But Sarah had a new vision. The question was whether she could get the procurement officer on board.

"Who do you actually work with to decide what you take out for procurement?" she asked him when they sat down together. "How do you start to build a strategy on what good procurement looks like in the tech sector?"

"I just wait for contracts to come up for renewal," he answered. "We put them out to market, we benchmark, and we award."

Sarah wasn't surprised by his answer. The tech industry at the time was less advanced than it is today, and it was easy for buyers to fall into a similar cycle. Nevertheless, she took the opening to push him.

"How do you know, then, that what you're doing is the right thing for the business?"

This time, he didn't have an immediate answer.

Now, Sarah made her ask: "How do you feel about giving me a view of everything that you have up for renewal in the next 18 months?" she asked him. "Let me take a look at what we could do creatively if we had a stab at *all* of it rather than having to wait to respond to each individual contract?"

The procurement officer eyed her from across the table, unconvinced. "We've got quite a good pattern in place," he said.

Sarah held her ground. For a moment neither of them spoke.

"Sure," he relented with a shrug. "You can give it a shot."

Getting him to agree had been a win, but Sarah didn't have an abundance of optimism. The procurement officer clearly felt that he had a perfectly good system in place, and it was possible he was right. Still, she was determined to see what she could find.

She got to work poring over the company's documents, trying to get a handle on their complex tech stack. As she sorted through everything, she began to spot some interesting patterns.

"I noticed that quite a few of their contracts overlapped," says Sarah. "I knew that we could create more efficiency by bringing them together into a single source supplier, which would allow the procurement team to go through a single procurement process."

When she finished her analysis, Sarah returned to the procurement officer. "I took a look at the information you shared, and I think I have some good news," she told him. "Based on your targets and what you need to achieve, I think you could improve your outcomes by 10-15% if you cut this overlap and start buying through a single source."

The procurement officer raised an eyebrow. Finally, she'd earned his full attention.

It was a creative move that resulted in a 300% growth margin in that account over two years. But for Sarah, the experience meant so much more. "That was the first time I was able to influence what an RFP would look like before it came to market," she says. "It was the first time we'd won a multi-architecture deal."

A lightbulb had flashed over her head.

"If we turn up a little bit differently and start thinking a little more creatively about what our customers are doing, why they're doing things the way that they are, and ask a few more questions that sit outside of the traditional RFP, we might be able to do more of these transformational deals," she thought to herself in awe.

The thought lit a fire beneath her.

The path forward seemed clear to Sarah. The biggest wins wouldn't come from the lowest-hanging fruit. Deals with real teeth could only result from taking a more thoughtful interest in how they could make a real difference for their customers.

Sarah called her team together.

She related the story of her success with the procurement officer: how she'd taken a step back, thought bigger, and ultimately been handsomely rewarded for her efforts.

"Yes, you might be successful now, chipping away at the low-hanging fruit," she told them. "But if we want to make a difference long-term, there are important extra things we can do."

Sarah figured that her win would have her team members lining up to follow in her footsteps. "I assumed that when I became a leader, I could just turn up and tell people how I'd been successful and then they'd all mirror that," she says with a laugh. "But I very quickly learned that this just isn't how leadership plays out."

Her sellers might have appreciated that she had a point, but it didn't mean they were convinced to change their approach. For those who were reliably hitting their quotas, the idea that they should start thinking more broadly and creatively seemed unnecessary at best and risky at worst. Taking a more deliberate approach with one customer would mean passing on the chance to score faster wins elsewhere.

"It's a very difficult thing for a salesperson to proactively walk away from a sale, particularly when they're chasing targets," Sarah says.

But she wasn't willing to let the idea go.

The way she saw it, sales effort couldn't be measured in wins alone. After all, chasing deals isn't free.

"It's easy to negate the fact that the cost-to-bid and cost-to-pursue are incredibly significant causes of burnt resources for any sales organization," she explains.

Thinking more critically about which deals they chased and how they chased them might do more than just get them bigger contracts, she reasoned: it might make them more efficient, too.

Her sellers might not have been jumping at her suggestion to be more intentional in the way they approached opportunities, but Sarah wasn't deterred.

One of her biggest priorities wasn't to force people to change their ways or come down hard on people who weren't doing what she felt was best. Instead, she threw her energy behind creating an environment that would encourage the behavior she wanted them to embrace.

"I wanted my team to be a safe place where someone could come and tell me, 'I don't think we should pursue this bid' without worrying that my reaction would be, 'Well, you aren't on target so if you aren't going after this bid, what are you doing?'"

On the contrary, Sarah knew open conversations about whether or not pursuing a bid was the right move were crucial to achieving her vision.

"There is so much value in having conversations around the qualification process and understanding the seller's decision not to bid," she says.

Instead, when a seller came to her with the decision not to chase a deal, she began choosing one of two responses:

---

1. Sometimes, it's enough to give them her nod of approval. "I agree with them and tell them they made the right call. I'll tell them they've saved us both time and money by not chasing something that wasn't a good fit."

---

2. Other times, it's an opportunity to get them to think about how they're approaching their customers. "I ask them: 'What would you have done differently earlier in the process if you had the chance to do this opportunity over?' The problem may well have been that we were simply too late to the table. If that was the issue, it's something we can learn from."

The more conversations the team had, the more it became apparent that the contracts they didn't bid for weren't necessarily a bad fit—often, they'd simply receive an RFP out of the blue instead of being a part of the creation process.

"If we shouldn't bid, it's probably because we haven't influenced early enough," says Sarah.

She knew that if they hadn't been involved in drafting the RFP, it meant someone else had been. Most enterprise RFPs are influenced either by an incumbent vendor or a preferred supplier, who helps shape the questions to their own benefit and narrow the path for potential competitors. Any time the team got an RFP they hadn't helped write, they were starting out on the back foot.

These conversations helped the team not only get better at qualification but also helped them think more about engaging with customers earlier and influencing their decision processes more. "It moved us from talking about qualification to talking about account planning more broadly. It moved us in the right direction," says Sarah.

In 2015, she got a chance to put this approach to the test.

An RFP landed on her desk. Two things about it made it interesting. First, the potential deal was a big one. Secondly, it was in a sector that the team believed would be a major area of growth for the business in the coming years: transport.

But the situation posed problems, too. Most obvious of them was the fact that it had come out of nowhere. "We were blind to it," says Sarah. "It hit us cold, and that's never a good place to be."

As she read through it, she was more discouraged. "We didn't influence early enough," she thought to herself as she reached the end of the document. What they were asking for wasn't a good fit. "This is probably one that we shouldn't bid on."

But letting a potentially great partnership slip away didn't seem like the right move, either.

The transport sector was a major priority for Sarah, so much so that she'd already created an A-team to focus on it. If they didn't bid on the first RFP that hit their inbox, they'd set a precedent that Sarah didn't want to set.

Ignoring the request wasn't an option. But bidding on something they couldn't win also didn't feel right. Sarah thought back to the curiosity that had made her a successful seller, and it was then that she alighted on a third plan: she contacted the company and asked for an informal session with its CIO.

When she sat down with the CIO, she didn't beat around the bush.

"We're really grateful recipients of the RFP," she told him. "But we're equally aware that we haven't had any prior conversations with you; we don't have a relationship. So I want to explore the background behind your RFP and understand what you're looking to achieve on a higher level."

Sarah wasn't trying to steer the executive in a particular direction. The way she saw it, the conversation would be a productive one regardless of how it ended. Even if she walked away still convinced that her team shouldn't bid, the executive would still know that he had been taken seriously.

No matter the outcome, she would be able to sow the seeds for a stronger relationship down the road.

The CIO told her that the RFP his company had released was actually only the first of many more to come. In fact, there'd be seven additional opportunities over the next five years, all of which would align with the theme of transformation within the sector. As he described the company's long-term vision for the coming years, Sarah saw clearly that she was in a great position to help, even if they weren't an ideal fit for the current RFP.

Sarah made a decision.

"Submit a bid," she told her team when she got back to the office. "Keep it in the context of the RFP and be respectful of what they ask. But more importantly, we need to develop a case for collaboration that shows them there's loads more we can do for them."

The proposal they compiled made their case clear: "We believe this is only the first of a few things that will come to market that support the transformation you're undertaking. And having observed what we think is happening in and around the market, this is what we think we can do, uniquely, to help you win business."

They sent in the documents. And waited.

The outcome was beyond their wildest dreams.

The Big Question:
How can you focus only on the deals that matter?

Sarah's bet paid off. "We built a brilliant relationship," she says. "I've never seen such a success story at a sector level. We won every RFP that came to market for the solution that we built. I'm so proud of the team."

And the success didn't end there. Thanks to Sarah's rigorous approach to qualification and uncompromising focus on relationship-building, her team created a foothold that grew by leaps and bounds.

Let's take a look at some of the numbers that defined their work in this sector over the next three years:

65%	3X	2X	+100
Growth	Funnel Improvement	Win Rate	Point improvement in Net Promoter Score (NPS)

Sarah sees evidence of the power of better relationships everywhere she looks, and the massive NPS improvement is one of her proudest achievements.

"NPS played a huge part in testing the value we were bringing to our relationships," she says. When she began, this business segment had a score that was a "market-leading terrible" -44. Just three years later, it was an outstanding +56.

"That's how much we could change customer sentiment just by being customer-centric," she says.

What does that look like in the real world? "First invest in what they want, then be really creative in the solutions that you deliver."

What makes qualification so important to account planning?

Your sellers' time and resources are finite. There's simply no way around it.

This means that for every action a rep takes, there are many other possible actions they're not taking. Consciously or not, every deal you chase is a decision to knock on one door at the expense of another.

Rigorous qualification is a foundational pillar of account planning because it's the only way to focus your attention on building real, mutually beneficial relationships. It's all about finding the deals that matter so you can have the maximum impact for both your business and your customer.

Chasing a high number of smaller, transactional deals might help a seller hit their quota for the quarter, but it won't create the kind of long-term partnerships that move you out of the status of being "just another vendor" and pay off in the long term.

When you select which deals to pursue carefully, however, you can hone in on the opportunities in which you're best positioned to help your customers succeed. Then, you can go all-in on aligning an account team, building an extensive roster of relationships, and becoming a strategic partner to your customers.

In other words, you'll have the time, resources, and focus to do real account planning.

Sarah isn't alone in her beliefs. When I spoke with Alison Greenwood, Regional Vice President and General Manager at Lumen, she told me that selective investment is almost always a winning strategy. "When you reduce the number of opportunities you're chasing, your win rate should increase," she said.

"Sellers can get a little bit optimistic," she adds. "We think that because we have all these features and because we have the right price, the customer will want our service. In reality, we need to be much more disciplined about getting deep into their business and deciding how to compete—and whether to compete at all. That, I think, is the foundation of account planning."

Account planning, as we all know by now, is rooted above all in putting your customer first. It requires teams to consider where and with whom they can have the greatest impact over the long term rather than where they can score a quick win.

Account planning only works when you invest real attention in your relationships, which can't be done if you're chasing every minor opportunity that comes your way. You have to take a bigger-picture, more thoughtful approach.

Sometimes, you have to say "No" to say "Yes."

Outcomes of good qualification include:

- Higher win rate percentage
- Bigger deals

- Shortened sales cycles with better ROI for your team's time and energy
- Better opportunities.

These outcomes come together in the ultimate success metric, called Sales Velocity, resulting in happier customers who get the attention and right-sized solutions that fit their strategic goals. We can think about it this way:

$$V = \frac{\#_{\text{QUALIFIED OPPORTUNITIES}} \times \$_{\text{DEAL VALUE}} \times \%_{\text{WIN RATE}}}{L_{\text{LENGTH OF SALES CYCLE}}}$$

V = SALES VELOCITY

Put simply, when you only go after deals you can (and should) win, you can confidently invest your time, effort, and resources into winning them.

How can you create a culture of thoughtful qualification and long-term thinking?

"It's scary to look at longer-term horizons when you've got quotas to hit in the short term," admits Sarah. "But it's worth it. I always told my sellers: Hold your nerve."

Set clear, short-term metrics

To keep her team on track, Sarah focused their attention on the kinds of performance metrics that indicated long-term success.

"If we believed in our plan and we had clear milestones, we'd know whether we're progressing and could redefine what success looks like," says Sarah.

"Thinking long-term didn't mean we were just waiting for a contract to land in two years. It was about creating the kinds of near-term proof points with metrics that kept people motivated and confident that they were doing the right things."

Don't make sellers afraid of saying "No"

Sarah knows that you can't ask people to turn away from short-term gains unless you make them feel safe doing so.

"The safety of the environment for people to talk about their customers, their planning, and their opportunities is really, really important," she says.

"If they think they're coming to a deal clinic to be judged on what they don't know rather than having a chance to talk about their ideas and gather feedback and insights from other people, you'll never get that opportunity to really qualify and optimize what each opportunity can do."

Balance science and art

"Everyone should look at sales through both the science and the art," Sarah says. "Because there is a real value in ensuring the two work in parallel."

"You could follow really rigorous qualification processes, but not think about how you present and turn up for your customers," she explains. "Alternatively, you could have really polished content but not be methodical in the way that you go about qualifying and planning. And I think those two, hand in glove, have to be part of any sales culture. Both have to be top-of-mind."

The four qualification questions sales teams should ask about every deal

There are only two reasons you lose a deal: either you were outsold, or you shouldn't have been there in the first place.

Good qualification is more than deciding whether you're in or you're out—it's about orienting your thinking around four core principles.

---

1. **Is there an opportunity?**

   This question may seem counterintuitive, but it's often overlooked, particularly when you're trying to expand within an existing account. What may look like a great path toward a more expansive relationship might end in a sneakily disguised dead-end if you don't know what to look for.

   Here's what you need to figure out before going all in:

   Is this initiative a priority for the customer?
   Your customers are being pulled in a million different directions, with unending wish lists of things they'd like to pursue. Is your project among the most important on the list? It's not always easy to tell.

   To find out, you'll need to figure out where and why the project began. Most importantly, you'll want to pinpoint which executive is backing the idea and whether you have an existing relationship. If there's support from on-high, you're far less likely to see interest fade.

   Do we understand their goals?
   What is your customer trying to do? What's stopping them from getting there? If the objectives are vague, you may be better off steering clear.

Do they have access to cash?

If there's no funding, there's no deal. Projects backed by executives and linked to key strategic objectives are the most likely to get the funding they need.

Is there a compelling event?

Why is the customer in the market for your solution right now? Is there a time-sensitive external or internal pressure? Is that pressure connected to key players within the account? Do they need to take an action, make a decision, solve a problem, or take advantage of an opportunity by a particular date?

Most importantly, have we validated these insights with the customer?

This is a critical question because answering it gives us insight into:

- Why they need to act
- The consequences of inaction
- Who is ultimately responsible for the outcome.

Account planning is all about aligning with our customers' goals. Knowing not only what the customer seeks to achieve but also how important they consider that objective to be is essential information when deciding whether a deal is worth pursuing.

---

2. **Can we compete?**

Art and science come together in this question. Determining how well you're positioned is a hybrid of technical capabilities and positioning. To answer this question, you'll need to consider:

What are their formal decision criteria?

How will your potential customer evaluate their options? What "must-have" parameters define their search? Do you fit them? Do you even know what they are? If you don't have that information, it might be a red flag with regard to the quality of the relationships you've built within the account.

Does our solution fit?

This question is black-and-white: an answer of "Yes" *must* link to those formal criteria.

Beyond that, though, it's valuable to know what key players within the organization consider to be their "must-haves." Match *what's* most important to *who's* most important. If you can do that, you'll be able to differentiate yourself and your solution.

Do you have a track record with this customer?

Have you worked with key people within the account before? What about suppliers? Partners? Are there previous projects either with this particular group or elsewhere in the organization that you can point to as grounds for trust?

What is your unique business value?

What do you have—that you know is important to the customer—that only you can provide? Be able to make a case for:

- *What* you're going to do
- *Why* it will help the customer rise to the challenge or opportunity presented by their compelling event
- *How much* it will impact their business (ROI)
- *Proof* you will be able to offer to measure success.

3. **Can we win?**

The size of the deal and the significance of the logo mean next to nothing if you don't stand a chance of winning in the first place.

Assessing this chance comes back to relationships. We'll take a deep dive into the importance of relationships in the next chapter, but at a glance, we can answer this question by considering whether you have the trust and backing of the people who matter.

What do power and influence look like within the organization?
One of the biggest reasons sellers lose deals is that they don't have access to people who can actually buy. You'll need to do some investigative work to uncover how power really flows within the organization.

Do we have support?
Will key players back and sell for us when we aren't there? Do we have people who will give us important information that we can use to advance the deal?

Do we have access to executives?
It's an often overlooked but supremely valuable piece of the puzzle.

What are their informal decision criteria?
There are technical specs, sure, but there are also less tangible influences on decision-making. How do decisions really get made? What isn't spelled out in the RFP?

4. **Is it worth winning?**

You can't chase everything that comes across your desk. Sometimes, you'll want to pass on an opportunity in favor of a more important pursuit. To separate the wheat from the chaff, ask your team:

Will we be successful with this project?
Will it be valuable for our customer? For us? Will it help us do more with this customer in the future?

Are our cultures compatible?
There's a wide range of workplaces out there, from highly structured bureaucratic organizations to those that encourage an entrepreneurial spirit; collaboration-focused groups to companies that prioritize the individual. Generally speaking, the best customer relationships stem from internal cultures that align with one another.

Will this contribute to our strategic growth?
How will this deal fit within your long- and short-term goals? Will it help you...

- Reach new markets?
- Keep out a competitor?
- Grow within the account?
- Grow your market share?
- Open new revenue streams?

Just because you *can* win a deal doesn't necessarily mean you should. If chasing something means pulling a seller away from a more fruitful investment of time and resources, or detracts from your purpose, culture, and focus, it can be more strategic to walk away.

These four key questions are best used to do more than simply qualify yourself in or out of a deal. At their most effective, these lines of inquiry can help you take a step back and consider how you might be able to make the deal in front of you more valuable for both you and the customer. In Sarah's experience, that meant taking an ill-fitting opportunity and growing it into a multi-deal partnership that allowed her to get ahead of competitors, influence RFPs, and spend her time on bigger, better deals.

As we've seen, the first step in good qualification comes from achieving good insight into your customer's goals and priorities, as we covered in Chapter 8. Now, in Chapter 9, we'll consider the other essential pillar: relationships.

"You can break down barriers faster simply by having knowledge."

Billy Martin
Senior Director of Leadership Development and Strategic
Enablement Programs, Medidata

9

Know Your Customer

Billy Martin is the Senior Director of Leadership Development and Strategic Enablement Programs at Medidata (a Dassault Systèmes company). He previously spent a decade at Salesforce, where he designed the programs completed by all new sales leaders and by all new company hires.

Pat Reilly is the Senior Director of Sales Field Enablement at Medidata. She's worked in sales and sales enablement for more than 30 years, previously at Random House and Hewlett Packard Enterprise.

Customers buy outcomes.

They aren't in the market for products or services; they aren't buying just to buy. They're on a mission to solve a problem, fill a gap, or capitalize on an opportunity.

The product or service you're selling is the method or tool they will use to get there.

Before you strategize how you're going to sell, therefore, you have to understand the organization you're selling to.

You need insights—into the business, its priorities, and its people—so you know:

- What problem you're going to solve
- What impact the solution will have for your customer

- What's standing in the way.

To better understand where insights come from and how teams can make them a pivotal part of their account planning strategy, I spoke with two veteran sales enablement leaders at Medidata: Billy Martin, Senior Director of Leadership Development and Strategic Enablement Programs, and Pat Reilly, Senior Director of Sales Field Enablement.

In this chapter, we break down how you can collaborate with both your team and your customers to get to the heart of the outcomes your customers want to achieve and how you can position yourself to deliver them.

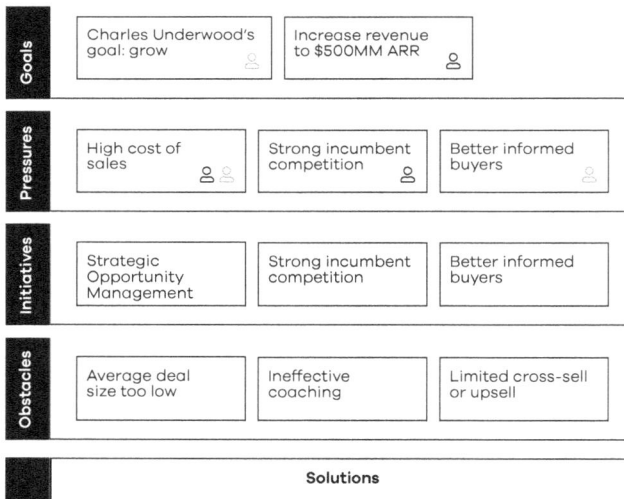

Goals	Charles Underwood's goal: grow	Increase revenue to $500MM ARR	
Pressures	High cost of sales	Strong incumbent competition	Better informed buyers
Initiatives	Strategic Opportunity Management	Strong incumbent competition	Better informed buyers
Obstacles	Average deal size too low	Ineffective coaching	Limited cross-sell or upsell
	Solutions		

Four essential insights

Picture seeing before you what looks like a great opportunity. You want to inspire the prospect to act by showing them what your solution will be able to do for them. But before you jump head-first into the sales process, there are four fundamental things you must know:

1. **What are their goals?**

    Goals are the big, bright North Stars that your customer is working toward. They are the end results that a company or a group within it needs to achieve. Serious goals will be both measurable and set against a particular timeframe. Often, they'll even be tied to executives' bonus payouts. All to say, they're a pretty big deal.

    A goal might be to...

    - Grow revenue by 10% over the next six quarters
    - Increase net new customers to 3,000 in 24 months
    - Expand market share from 30% to 50% in the next five years.

    Notice that each one of these examples includes both a measurable result and a time in which that result needs to be achieved.

2. **What pressures are forcing the customer to act?**

    A *pressure* is anything that has a direct impact on your customer's ability to reach their goals.

    It could be rooted either internally or externally. It might be operational, financial, or technical, or have to do with markets, competitors, partners, suppliers, or even their own customers.

    What's putting the squeeze on your customer's key decision-makers? Why do they need to act? Who will benefit if they do?

    "One of the most important things in our go-to-market strategy is understanding pressures. We call them the 'tipping point'—the thing that is pushing somebody to change the status quo," says Billy.

A pressure might be...

- Losing market share to a competitor
- Supplier costs rising
- Insufficient revenue.

Identifying pressures is often a process of narrowing broad, industry-based assumptions down to the particular challenges facing your customer.

"For my team, the pressures facing companies in the life sciences are fairly similar for everybody. So we work to illuminate those for our sellers so they have a jumping-off point," explains Billy. "It's their job to take those and do some digging to find out what pressures are manifesting uniquely for a particular account. A pressure driving one company might not impact another."

It's also worth getting a handle on the context surrounding the pressure your customer faces. How long has it been there? Why hasn't it been fixed before? Was it because no one knew how to solve it? Lack of resources? Perhaps no one even realized it was there?

---

3. **What initiatives are they undertaking to relieve those pressures?**

An *initiative* is a project your customer is undertaking (or planning to undertake) in order to overcome their pressures and meet their goals.

An initiative could be to...

- Streamline a core business process
- Improve the product release cycle
- Recruit better talent.

As you think about initiatives, it's important that you place yourself firmly in your customer's shoes. What language do they use to talk about the project? What time constraints are they working within?

Most importantly, you'll need to assess how important this initiative is for the organization. Companies have an endless list of things they want to achieve and projects they want to tackle, but most never come to fruition. Your customer can't fund every project. Make sure the one you're ready to help with is a member of the chosen few.

---

4. **What obstacles stand in their way?**

An *obstacle* is an internal problem.

The enemy might be an operational issue rooted in organization, process, culture, skill, or tech. It could also be that something is broken, suboptimal, or even non-existent.

Obstacles might include...

- Outdated technology
- Weak planning methods
- Excessive time to get resources.

Whatever it is, be sure that the obstacle you identify is something tangible. That way, you can point to a specific way that your solution will help your customer overcome it. Remember: risk appears when you don't know exactly what you're trying to achieve.

How can you gather these insights?

Knowing what your customer's goals, pressures, initiatives, and obstacles are matters, but this level of deep understanding doesn't come easy. The importance of qualifying your deals is on full display here, because sellers can only invest their precious time and resources in so many places.

Once you know where to focus, it's all about leaning into the natural curiosity that makes sellers good at what they do.

Do your research

Research is the name of the game. At this phase, places as accessible as company websites and LinkedIn feeds are your friends, as well as data captured in your CRM.

When gathering business insights, ask:

- What are this organization's major markets? Who do they sell to? Why are they successful?
- Who are their competitors and how do they stack up against them?
- What has their profit and revenue looked like in recent years?
- Have they acquired any other companies recently? Merged? Sold off a piece of the business?
- Have there been any recent changes in executive leadership?
- Which business units are succeeding and growing?
- What goals and pressures are impacting your target group?
- What's standing in their way?

This kind of information might seem table stakes, but having a firm grasp on these key facts will set you apart.

"Most salespeople are strong on knowing what their product and solution can do," says Billy "But they're weak when it comes to really understanding the business drivers in the industries they sell into."

When I spoke with Allison Greenwood, Regional VP and General Manager at Lumen, she agreed wholeheartedly.

"Building a relationship with a customer based on a deep understanding of their business becomes, in and of itself, a differentiator," she told me. "Even if your product isn't the perfect product, you can still win if you're aligned with their business. They're going to see you differently, and you'll have an inroad to so many more opportunities if you aren't like everyone else who is showing up only with their feature and flavor of the day. It's a 10x factor approach."

Work as a team

As with every aspect of account planning, sellers will be most successful if they approach insight-gathering as a team.

"When you collaborate, you're getting the big picture," says Billy. "What's driving that business to make decisions? Remember: we're trying to get them to change the way they do things—sometimes radically. And that needs to be in the context of the true pressures that exist in their industry. So it's critical to figure that stuff out as a team."

By gathering people both within the sales team and beyond it, you can tap into a wide variety of viewpoints, each with a unique perspective on the industry and the customer.

For Pat, this collective knowledge is foundational to success.

"From the beginning, I tell my sales teams that they need to know everything they can about their customer, and they need to leverage everyone on their team to do that," she says. "But I also make sure they know that they don't have to know everything at once. As people bring their different insights back to a shared collaboration point, you'll start to reveal the customer's true situation."

"It's almost like a puzzle: A picture is going to reveal itself, and you don't know what it's exactly going to be, but it's going to be valuable and it's going to keep you aligned with your customer," says Pat. "Once you look at all the insights collectively, you have a much bigger story than you would have had individually. All of these little pieces of information add up to something big."

In centralizing the output of everyone's communications, Billy says, you'll get where you want to go more quickly. "There's a speed-to-market advantage in getting more people engaged in the process," he says. "You can break down barriers faster simply by having knowledge."

But collaboration runs deeper than that—and offers much more potential.

"The most valuable thing you can offer your customers is your wide breadth of solutions," explains Billy. "People in your organization are responsible for different verticals and solutions, and by getting everyone involved in the conversation, you can crack open the doors and construct a more holistic approach—one that will speak to the executive level of the company. Instead of getting stuck working with a single department, you can move higher."

Getting all hands on deck can improve both the breadth and the quality of your relationships.

"We all know that, in sales, the higher we can get in an organization, the more likely we are to build a trusted advisor relationship," says Billy. "The ability to get higher only happens when different stakeholders come together."

Build an insight map.

Having a firm understanding of your customer's goals, pressures, initiatives, and obstacles is good. Gathering these insights in one place is far, far better.

When you put everything together, you get what we call an insight map.

"An insight map is the major collaboration point where everybody comes together to share what they know," says Pat. "When everybody brings their individual insights to one central location, you can start to see how they all fit together."

An insight map allows you to consolidate your customer's strategic priorities in one place. And, most importantly of all, requires that you start assessing how you can help.

Insight Map

"Your sellers should be helping your customers solve problems and achieve their goals," Pat says. "The insight map is where you're going to do it."

Building an insight map is a valuable exercise for sellers because it...

- ☑ Forces you to think from the customer's perspective; it's impossible to create or discuss an insight map without focusing on the customer
- ☑ Shows you what is important and what is driving key players
- ☑ Earns you the privilege of having strategic conversations at higher levels of the organization.

After you create an insight map, you're left with a concise and insightful document that you can take to the star of the show: your customer.

Validate what you know

Solo research and internal collaboration are essential first steps, but no set of insights is complete until you've spoken with the actual people whose goals, pressures, initiatives, and obstacles you're trying to understand.

"Ultimately, your insight map is the basis for customer conversations," says Pat. "Sales is all about conversations. We want to have as many conversations as we possibly can across the entire organization. Showing up with insights earns us the right to do that."

"The problems we solve are complex," adds Billy. "So it was a key revelation for us that getting our sellers to collaborate, not only with the internal team but also with the client, was an absolute necessity."

Take your insight map to your customer. It won't be perfect, but if you've managed to get most of the way there, you'll be able to have a more productive conversation that will build trust and begin to position you in their eyes as more than "just another vendor."

"This is your opportunity to bring these insights to your customer and say, *'I've been researching your company and your industry and having lots of conversations with my colleagues. Can we take a few minutes to discuss what we're seeing; maybe get you to validate it?'*" says Pat. "What that does is elevate you in their eyes. You're not just a vendor, you're someone who is invested in their industry and their success."

"I always ask my reps: Do you feel that it's important to illuminate the sales process for the client?" says Billy. "Everyone will say, *'Of course—the more you can illuminate the sales process and collaborate on a mutual win plan, the better.'* You don't keep the client in the dark about the opportunity, so why would you keep them in the dark when it comes to your success planning or growth plan? That's not something you do in a vacuum. The client has to be involved."

Ideally, the conversation you have with your customer about your insight map won't just prove that you understand their business. It should also bring them new information— or a new vantage point through which to understand it.

"You may actually know more than they do, because they're in their silos, whereas you've spread out across their company," explains Pat. "You're bringing them a bigger picture than they might actually have, all built from those little bits and pieces that you've been putting together."

Linking people and problems

The organization might be the one facing the problem or working toward the goal, but it's the individuals within the company who will either act or feel the pain.

It's essential to know who's behind the insights you've uncovered and how they'll be impacted by the solution you're offering.

You can start by getting a handle on who owns what.

- **Goals** are the domain of the executive; it's these leaders who are responsible for the big-picture objectives that guide the activities of the team
- **Pressures** are felt by executives and in turn passed on to management; it's then management's job to figure out what to do about them

- **Initiatives** are the projects that management puts in place to respond to the pressures and reach the goals of their executive bosses
- **Obstacles** are the challenge of tech and operations folks who are tasked with figuring out how to overcome them in order to implement the solution successfully.

When you take your insights to a customer, it's important that you put them in the context of the person with whom you're meeting. Don't waste your breath talking about goals with someone tactical, and don't get into the weeds on the details with someone whose energy is devoted to the big picture. Always keep your sights set on who you're speaking to and what matters to them.

Creating an insight-driven culture

Billy sees sales teams that excel at insight-building as a product of good coaching and strong leadership.

"Making insights part of your sales culture has to be a leaders-first approach," he says. "It's a coaching effort from the top down."

Usually, the challenge is simply to help sellers stick with it long enough to see the value.

"Sellers can get a little loosey-goosey when it comes to the planning part of sales," he says. "But when they devote their time to building out their insights, they reap massive benefits. Their leaders need to steer them in the right direction and help them see what's in it for them. When we can draw a clear line that connects all the research they're doing and the effort they're putting to the ultimate, closed-won opportunity, people start to see why this stuff matters."

Coaching sellers, he believes, is a lot like coaching athletes. "It's easy to coach once you're on the field, but it's the behind-the-scenes planning and preparation that gets you there and puts you in a position to win."

To help his reps get in tip-top selling shape, he requires them to consider themselves what he dubs "GM of My Business." "The idea is that sellers must be able to articulate all the key drivers influencing the companies within their territory or for a particular client. And they must do so through an insight map."

Billy believes that training sellers to prioritize insights is a process that can be taught. "And if you can teach it, you can coach it," he reasons. "Most professionals have coaches. They practice every day. But salespeople don't usually do that. We need to make sure that they practice enough that they embed those skills in their DNA."

Six best practices for effective insights

As you guide your teams to prioritize business insights, orient their work around six fundamentals that will ensure that their knowledge is sturdy, accurate, and create mutual value for your organization and for your customer.

---

1. Tell a logical story. Know what your customer is trying to achieve, how they're trying to achieve it, and why.

---

2. Ensure every goal and pressure is both specific and tied to a timeframe.

---

3. Validate and triangulate what you know. Work with a broad team within your organization to bring together

all of the information that is available. Then confirm and deepen those insights with your customer.

4. Know who is responsible for or impacted by each goal, pressure, initiative, and obstacle.

5. Confirm that the initiatives you're positioned to support are priorities for your customer. Know why your customer has chosen to pursue them over every other project that could have claimed their attention.

6. Define every obstacle so you know exactly what your customer is trying to overcome and what success will look like.

Your customers' businesses are complicated and the industries in which they work are constantly evolving. Your buyers are up against a slew of complex pressures and are working toward challenging goals. When your sellers can show up with knowledge and insight, they'll be able to establish themselves as serious, trustworthy partners.

Insights are the base that supports the development of great relationships. And as we'll see in the coming chapter, mastering relationships is what will take your account planning to the next level.

"No one operates alone."

Sarah Bennett
Vice President of Global Finance and Revenue Operations,
Informatica

10

Reaching the People Who Matter

Sarah Bennett leads market operations and enablement as Vice President of Global Finance and Revenue Operations at Informatica. She has served in various sales leadership roles over the course of her career at Conga, McAfee, and Dell/EMC, including director of sales finance and chief of staff for sales strategy, planning, and programs.

Every story we've told in this book has the same fundamental principle at its core: the power of relationships. No matter what you're trying to achieve with a customer, you'll be doomed to a Sisyphean existence if you don't know—or have the trust of—the people who matter within their organization.

Sarah Bennett puts this idea front and center in her position overseeing global revenue operations and enablement at Informatica. "We always have to remember that people buy from people," she says. "That fact is absolutely essential."

And it's more important now than ever before. "Selling isn't about your product and its features and functions anymore," Sarah explains. "It's about understanding your customers' challenges and figuring out what you can do to support them."

In its most basic application, this means having a strong handle on your personas. But even in that case, account planning demands that you think more deeply.

"Yes, our personas tend to be CIOs, CDOs, CROs, and other executives, but we can't just think about them as individual people. No one operates alone. Particularly when it comes to those who occupy that level of the business, they're surrounded by support. So it's not just the CIO we have to think about—it's the *office* of the CIO and everyone who supports the chain."

In fact, it's those in supporting positions who often yield the most fruitful relationships. "It's the roles underneath those heads of office that we often align most of our relationships with," says Sarah.

Building a wide range of relationships is critical because decisions don't happen in a vacuum. "Within any organization, there will be those who can influence and those who can mentor," says Sarah. "And there will also usually be those who are not supporters at all."

"As part of building relationships, we have to pay attention to their background and history. Do they have any allegiances to our competitors? What does the political dynamic inside the business look like? If we understand hierarchies and relationships, we can get to the person we *really* need to reach."

What happens when sellers don't prioritize relationships?

Casting a wide net and prioritizing deeper understanding can feel uncomfortable for sellers.

"Salespeople like to feel like they control a deal in its entirety," says Sarah. "Less experienced sellers sometimes prioritize that feeling of control over building important relationships, and it doesn't often end well."

One rep she worked with was chasing a net-new deal. The opportunity was a substantial one, but still, the seller was only working with a few people in the account.

To help move the deal forward, the rep was offered the support of an executive sponsor.

"We see a lot of value in building relationships between our executives and leaders within our customers' businesses," says Sarah. "If we can initiate those relationships early enough in the process, they often end up having really beneficial conversations because they're often up against the same challenges."

But the rep turned down the opportunity to bring in executive support. "He felt like doing so would expose him," explains Sarah. "He thought it would mean that someone else would be meddling in his deal and that he would lose control of the situation."

Instead of having someone with gravitas on his side who could speak, peer-to-peer, with his potential customers, the rep decided to go it alone. He also stuck to the product-centric approach that he had been using from the start. He spent his time talking about what his solution would be able to do for the customer rather than getting to the heart of what the customer wanted to achieve.

Ultimately, unable to build the trust and alignment within the account that he needed, the rep lost the deal.

"I know that if he had engaged our CIO, we absolutely would have made it," says Sarah. "We may not have won the deal in its entirety, but we certainly wouldn't have lost it at the extreme that we did."

What happens when sellers *do* prioritize relationships?

A different salesperson was working on another deal. Knowing the importance of building a wide network of support and connection within the account, he called a wider account team together to review the opportunity and explore the chances they might have to strengthen their ties.

One meeting invitee was the CRO. Not long after reviewing the map of key people—both known and unknown—within the account, the CRO spoke up.

"Wait," he said, pointing at one of the figures on the screen. "I know him! We've worked together in the past."

The account owner immediately saw the value in the connection.

"That would be a really important person to have on our side," the rep said. "Would you be willing to help me build that relationship?"

The CRO agreed. The two former colleagues reconnected, and not long after, the team won the deal.

The Big Question:
Who matters and how can you build trust with them?

Two relationship mistakes doom deals:

1. You don't sell to the people who will ultimately make the decision.
2. You don't understand what matters to them.

To avoid these pitfalls, you'll need to ensure that your sellers develop strong relationships with as many of the right people within an organization as they can.

How do you know whether you're connecting with the right people?

When I spoke with Phil Trapani of Upland Altify, he told me that the only thing worse than no relationships is getting distracted by the wrong ones.

"You have to be able to connect with the people who matter," he said. "And I choose those words carefully because a lot of sellers connect with the wrong people or have trouble connecting with the people who actually drive decisions."

Getting distracted by stakeholders without influence can derail your progress. Here's how to stay on track:

Get involved early

Building trust takes time, which is one of the critical reasons that influencing the buying process early yields so many more rewards than showing up halfway through.

Executives tend to be involved at the start and end of the buying process, which means that by the time many sellers become involved in a deal, it's difficult to reach the people who hold the most sway. Most of the important decisions about what an organization is looking for have already been made.

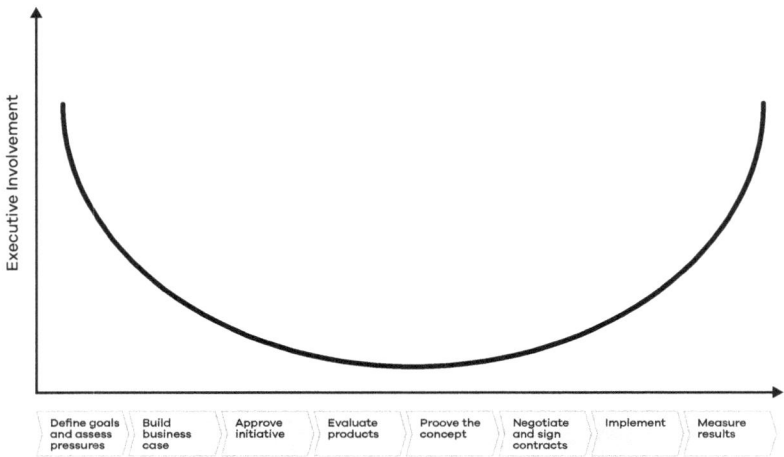

Executives tend to be heavily involved in the early stages of a buying cycle. Arriving late means missed opportunities to work with them.

As we saw in the previous chapter, if you don't influence early, you're almost always condemning yourself to start the sales process on the back foot. But if you're able to build important relationships early, you'll have an outsized impact on the entire process.

Look beyond the org chart and consider internal politics

Traditionally, sellers have known to find the person in charge. Who owns the budget? Who has the power to give the nod or kill the deal?

The executives who have the authority to make decisions are still hugely important, but it's not enough to focus on them alone.

Instead, salespeople should be on the lookout for all the ways influence can manifest within an organization. Naturally, it travels down the organizational chart from leaders to their subordinates, but it can also move laterally, or even upwards.

"The CDO might be the buyer persona we sell to, but in reality, they aren't working alone," says Sarah. "They're not going to do all the work and make all the decisions. That means we want to see who else is involved. Where's the budget owned? Is it with the business or is it with IT? What other lines of business are going to be impacted by this decision?"

A member of an organization's political structure might be someone who at first glance appears to be insignificant, but who has the trust and respect of someone with material power. That person's opinion may go a long way, and failing to account for them could end up being a stumbling block down the road.

Tap into your extended revenue team

Especially when you're looking to expand within an existing account, it's important to remember that your company's relationships with your customer extend far beyond the sales team.

"If we get implementation people, partner teams, customer success managers, even support people, involved, they can update us on the conversations they're having and we can bring all the information we have together," says Sarah.

Often, these other customer-facing teams have invaluable insights into your customer's inner-workings. They can alert you to how people are connected, who holds sway, and what values are driving those in charge.

Don't get single-threaded

It can be tempting to find an ally within an account and cling to them. But having a small circle of contacts is a dangerous game.

Your champion could leave for another job, or turn out not to have the authority they'd led you to believe. Alternatively, there may be a supremely influential person lurking just out of sight who is actively working against you. Just because you don't see someone doesn't mean they aren't there.

When I spoke with Travis Hill of Upland Altify, he told me that this problem is a common one.

Travis once worked with General Electric to bring account planning to a group of sellers who sold technology and parts to the train industry. A series of new software innovations had, nearly overnight, transformed both what and to whom the team needed to sell.

The sellers were veterans. "The average person on the team had been there for 15-plus years and worked the same accounts for more than a decade—some for almost 20 years," says Travis.

He started out by asking them about their accounts. "They knew them inside and out," he remembers.

"I've been with this customer for 10 years," one rep told him. "I know everyone I need to know."

But when Travis asked the sellers to build relationship maps that laid out exactly where they had contacts, the cracks in their conviction began to appear.

Travis looked at one of the maps a seller had built. "This looks like a pencil," he told the group bluntly. "You know the COO, the VP and director of operations, and that's it. Some of you have five or six people listed, but it's still a pencil:

straight up and down. What happens if somebody leaves? What happens if the chain breaks?"

Travis still remembers how quickly the blood drained from the sellers' faces.

Create a visual map of your relationships

Looking at a visual can help your team see their relationships more clearly.

"You're going to be selling software now," he told the room. "Who's buying that? Not the operations person you usually deal with. It's going to be the VP of IT—but who does that person report to?"

The sellers weren't sure.

"No idea? So you're telling me that you think you can develop a strategy for an account in which you'll have to sell to the IT team, but you don't even know who oversees them? That means you can't possibly know what's really important to them."

He could practically see the light bulbs snapping on above the veteran sellers' heads as they considered the empty spaces on the map.

Sarah also uses visual tools to help her sales teams stay on track.

"We use maps to create placeholders for people we don't know, but who we know we need to know," says Sarah. "It helps us drive toward building the relationships we need." For example, the CFO should always be shown somewhere— after all they are the person signing the checks! And don't forget those procurement people and understanding their MBOs.

"And as we add more and more to our relationship map, it's almost as if we're connecting the dots within the organization. We often look at it and say, *'Oh wow, this guy knows these three people? That's valuable information.'"*

On the flip side, a visual relationship map can also expose risk.

"One of the first things I look at is simply how many people a seller has on their map," Sarah says. "If I see that you don't have very many people, I immediately know that you're putting yourself in danger." Conversely, too many people could mean you are spending too much time with the wrong people, so be thoughtful about this.

Taking relationships from red to green

Finding the people who matter is one thing—getting them on your side is another. When key contacts on your relationship map aren't supporters, it's your job to figure out how to change their stance.

Figure out why they're against you

Do they have a bad history with a different product of yours? Do they feel threatened by how your solution might impact their role? Lean on your wider account team for context and background that can help you understand what's driving their opinions.

Empower supportive influencers

Internal colleagues are often much more compelling than external sellers. Understanding political ties within an account can help you identify who can help make your case. Which supporters influence this detractor? How can you help arm them to sell in your absence?

When I spoke with Alison Greenwood, Regional Vice President and General Manager at Lumen, she told me that building wide-reaching relationships is part of how she

measures success. "The #1 performance indicator I'm looking for is quality meetings with appropriate stakeholders,"
she explained. "Who are the really important folks at different layers of the business? Those meetings are really, really
important."

Return to selling value

"When I see red on the map, I always tell my sellers to go
back to proving value," says Sarah. "We need to show them
that we're not just here to push a product. Let's understand
their business challenges and then connect key people with
references who can speak to a relevant use case or an executive sponsor who has real credibility on the subject."

Five questions to help sellers develop better relationships

1. **Who matters and what role do they play?**
   Influential people are usually evident by their position
   in an org chart, but sometimes, people with pull can be
   harder to spot.

   Influence might take the form of being a trusted voice
   in the ear of a decision maker, or being a leading member
   of an important project.

   For each significant player, identify whether
   they're a(n):

   - Approver
   - Decision-maker
   - Evaluator
   - User.

Knowing what role they play can help you think about what relationship you need to build, what information you need to understand from them, and where they fit in your effort to build or expand a lasting partnership.

Remember: org charts might look similar, but every organization's political dynamics are unique. Getting to the heart of these dynamics is where the magic happens.

---

2. **What do they care about and how do they think?**
    What motivates the important people within the account? What traits define their personality and decision-making style? What do they value? Are they excited by or wary of change? What big priorities or challenges define their professional life right now, and what do they stand to gain or lose?

---

3. **What is their level of support for us?**
    Are they actively selling in your absence? Neutral? Actively advocating for your competitor? Somewhere in between? Knowing where you stand with each key player is essential to accurately assessing where you stand.

---

4. **To whom do we currently have access? What is the relationship gap?**
    Mapping out who you know can help you notice who's missing. That's where the danger lies. Just because you don't know anything about a particular member of an account doesn't mean they aren't there, nor that they aren't playing a role. Whether they're an enthusiastic supporter or diehard detractor, it's crucial that you have the full picture so you can figure out where to go next.

You should also consider how often you're in contact with the people you know. Are you speaking with them often enough to stay top-of-mind and keep up with how things are progressing?

---

5. How can we bridge the gap?

Reconciling your relationship gaps can take a variety of forms. You might get an introduction from someone else within the account. Or, you might turn to your own extended account team to determine whether someone on a customer-facing team—or even, as we saw earlier in this chapter, an executive—might have a connection you didn't know about.

Relationships are the lifeblood of account planning. They're how you build trust, how you understand your customers' goals, and how you break away from being "just another vendor."

But not all relationships are created equal. Too few connections—or those built with people who lack influence— have little value. Your team's goal should always be to stay focused on finding the people who matter and getting them on your side.

I've never seen an organization put a good account planning practice in place without good software to support them.

Phil Trapani
Upland Altify

11

Support and Scale
with Technology

Behind every elite sales team, there's an elite tech stack.

It's usually the people who get the glory when we talk about account planning—and rightly so. As we've seen again and again over the course of this book, the human relationships you build, both internally and with your customers, are what allow you to break away from being "just another vendor."

But to empower your team to do the hard and rewarding work of account planning, you must first give them the tools for the job.

The magic of account planning technology comes from its ability to translate the big account planning principles we've been talking about into real, day-to-day activities that can be carried out by your revenue teams.

But not all software is created equal.

So how do you choose? What role should tech play in your account planning organization? How can you maximize your new software's adoption and impact? We'll cover these questions and more in this chapter.

Why do sales leaders invest in account planning technology?

I've encountered a great number of sales leaders in the early stages of their search. Each has a vision for account planning that is unique to their organization, but their motivations tend to fall into these *three* buckets:

---

1. **Reaching predictable revenue growth** by increasing their pipeline and retention in key strategic accounts.

---

2. **Increasing win rates** by identifying and qualifying the right deals, aligning with their customers, and increasing sales velocity.

---

3. **Improving their forecast accuracy** by building a consistent and repeatable sales process.

In other words, they need to bring the full power of account planning to life. They need to feel more certain about the outcomes of their strategic efforts. Then they need to scale those outcomes across their organization.

What does account planning technology do?

Technology, in a word, makes account planning thrive.

As we saw in Chapter 4, though, it should never be mistaken as a substitute for methodology or good selling. It's a tool, not a strategy.

Without the principles in place to organize and orient your sales team and a commitment across the business to embrace a new way of working, even the best technology won't spark meaningful change.

What an account planning technology *will do* is create the conditions in which account planning can thrive.

Implemented alongside the approaches we've covered thus far, technology is an essential prerequisite for fully realized account planning. "To be honest," says Phil Trapani of Upland Altify, "I've never seen an organization put a good account planning practice in place without good software to support them."

That's because the right tech will:

- ☑ **Keep sellers on track** by bringing your organization's best practices into their daily sales motions
- ☑ **Encourage collaboration** across teams by centralizing information and offering actionable guidance
- ☑ **Foster more, better relationships** by helping teams see who they know, who they should know, and what key members of the account want and need
- ☑ **Drive more pipeline and higher-velocity sales** by visualizing whitespace, insights, and deal progress
- ☑ **Make sellers' jobs easier and more efficient** because it is simple to use and quick to adopt across the organization.

How do you choose the right account planning software?

Choosing the right piece of technology can feel like a minefield. There is no shortage of options, each one claiming its own superiority. What's right?

The answer comes back, of course, to what you need the software to do. As we've seen, account planning requires large-scale buy-in. It requires collaboration. It requires changing the way you build relationships with your customers at every level. The software you choose should be built to make all these things possible.

But what does that look like in practice? To sort the duds from the winners keep an eye out for *seven* critical features.

---

1. **Space for collaboration to bring teams together**

   Account planning is bigger than a single seller—and even than the sales team itself. If your tech keeps salespeople in their silos, you'll struggle to bring in the people they'll need from across the organization who can share insights, work through blockers, and create plans to further nurture your relationship with customers.

   Truly collaborative software is built to share information using your own common language. It should help facilitate group planning sessions and allow everyone to get a clear view of where you stand with an account or a particular opportunity and review as a team to improve your approach.

---

2. **In-app coaching and guidance to keep people on track**

   We saw in Chapter 4 that sales approaches can't just be taught in a classroom. Even the best trainings won't stick if their teachings aren't reinforced.

   But you can't ask sales managers to stand over their teams all day to make sure they're doing as they're told. That's where your account planning software can step in and pick up the slack.

   "It's pretty hard to get any good, consistent results without best practice account planning methods laid out within your technology," says Phil. "I can say that as a sales leader myself, I used to undervalue the benefit of in-product guidance. Well, shame on me. It makes an enormous difference."

Technology can offer simple nudges to keep sellers on the right track, and automatically alert them when things don't look right. By prompting reps about what questions to ask, which steps to take, and how to know whether their relationships are healthy, account planning software can get ahead of potential problems and remind your sales team of the nuances of account planning best practices that they may otherwise overlook.

---

3. **Visualization for better understanding**

    Numbers on a spreadsheet or notes in a slide deck are all well and good, but there's no substitute for being able to clearly see the state of people, problems, and potential that define an account.

    Know your people

    Who do you know? How do they influence one another? How do they feel about you? These insights are crucial for account planning because they allow you to see how strong your relationships are within an account.

    Relationship mapping gives sellers an immediate snapshot of how strong their position is with the people who matter, and where they may need to work harder to build trust and win support.

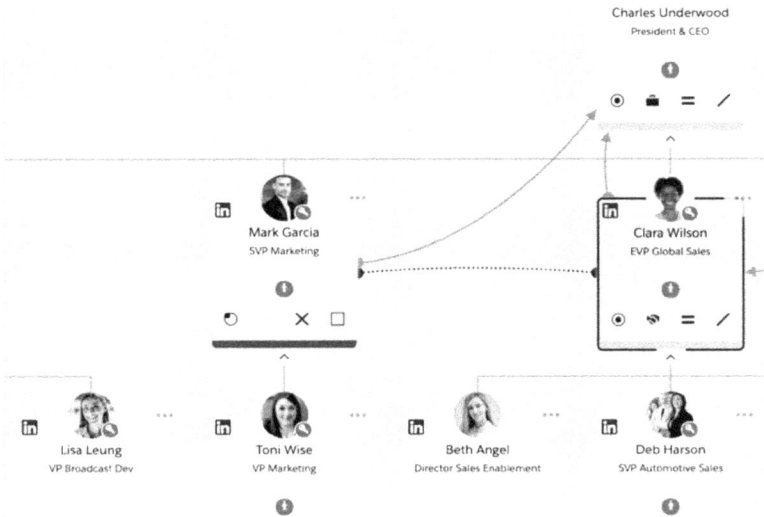

Who's on your side? Who's working against you? Who really pulls the strings? Seeing this information represented visually makes it more compelling and easier to share. A sparsely populated map can also raise alarm bells for a sales manager, allowing them to see at a glance that the team hasn't connected with as many people as it needs to.

See their problems
Mapping insights helps keep the objective of advancing customer interests top-of-mind.

Visualizing the customer's key goals, the pressures impacting these goals, and the initiatives that are currently in play to advance them allows anyone to get a bird's-eye view of how well you're serving your customers.

When I spoke with Travis Hill of Upland Altify, he told me that in his experience, seeing your information can make all the difference. "Once you have a technology that can present what you know visually, you can start seeing the gaps in your strategy."

This kind of visualization can even help drive conversations with customers themselves. Sharing an insight map with a customer and simply asking, *"Do we have this right?"* can help start a productive conversation that gets you aligned and strengthens your partnership.

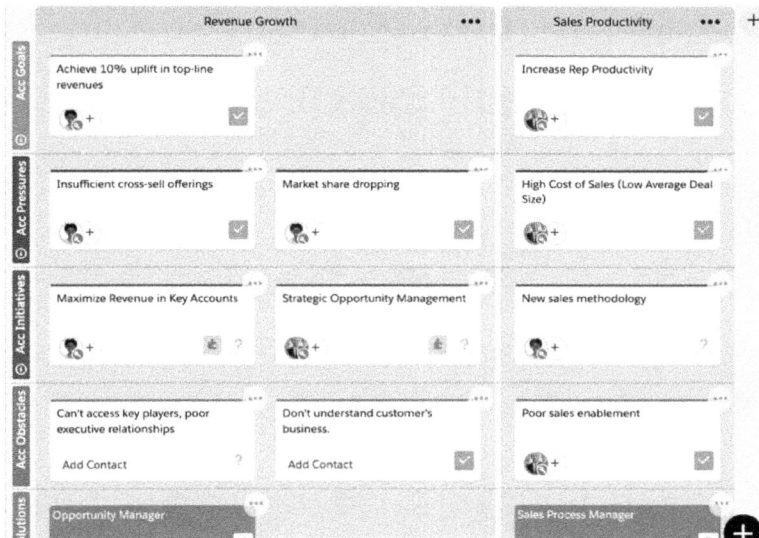

Map your potential

Visualization is also valuable when it comes to uncovering whitespace within an account.

Where have your solutions already been deployed? Are there others that would help advance your customer's goals? Or, perhaps, are there other teams or business units within your customer's organization that might benefit from the same solutions?

Mapping coverage gaps is the perfect starting point for discussions about how you can grow within an existing account.

"Visual feedback is so important because it's so much simpler to see green, yellow, and red than it is to try to describe the status of your work," says Phil. "I've had conversations in which I asked a seller, *'What do we know about this customer?'* only to immediately see, *'Holy s***, the map is blank. We clearly know nothing.'* On the flip side, if a seller can pull up an insight map with three or four goals that a particular person cares about, I know we're on the right track."

	TOTAL		Account Mgr ⊕		Conversation... ⊕	
▼ Ancaster Inc	$9.20M	7	$4.40M	3		
	$4.48M	14	$1.60M	4	$0.47M	2
	$1.06M	4	$0.41M	1	$0.10M	1
Ancaster Inc Parent	$2.10M	3	$0.40M	1		
♟ ♣ s ▾	$1.30M	5			$0.47M	2
	$1.06M	4	$0.41M	1	$0.10M	1
Ancaster Engineering ⊕	$2.60M	2	$1.00M	1		
♟ ♣ s ▾	$2.29M	5	$1.45M	2		
		0				
Ancaster Commodities ⊕		0				
♟ s ▾ ◑	$0.21M	3	$0.15M	2		
		0				
Ancaster Services	$4.50M	2	$3.00M	1		
♟ ♣ s ▾	$0.68M	1				
		0				
PLAN TOTAL	$9.20M	7	$4.40M	3	·	0
	$4.48M	14	$1.60M	4	$0.47M	2
	$1.06M	4	$0.41M	1	$0.10M	1

4. Simplicity for easy and sustained adoption

Software is only powerful if it's actually used. It's crucial to make it easy, then, for sales leaders and their supporting teams to hit the ground running. A piece of technology that requires learning an entirely new sales vocabulary or asks users to jump through hoops will have trouble catching on.

Phil puts it bluntly and best: "If the technology is too hard to use, salespeople just aren't going to use it."

The right technology will make sellers' jobs easier, not harder. It should simplify their organization, their insights, and their ability to collaborate, not feel like administrative busywork. When it checks these boxes, you'll be able to scale quickly.

"In my experience, implementing new software is infinitely easier if it genuinely makes sellers better at their jobs," says Phil. "Once sellers find out how easy and useful it is, it goes from '*What are they asking me to learn now?*' to '*Man, you're an idiot if you aren't using this.*'"

---

5. Adaptability to fit your teams

A rigid technology might seem like the easiest bet, but one size will never fit all. Your software should conform to whatever methodologies and best practices make sense for your organization, or even for an individual team. Look for software that will:

- ☑ Allow you to configure your own KPIs and other measurements
- ☑ Integrate with the analytics tools you already have in place
- ☑ Be compatible with the sales methodology you use
- ☑ Be right-sized for every go-to-market approach, from territory plans and big strategic global account plans to those for the mid-market and beyond.

---

6. Salesforce-native to start with data

Tech catches on when it lives where your sellers do. Salesforce is the central hub of most sales teams, so it's essential that your account planning software be there, too. Being built into Salesforce and 100% native allows your software to contextualize insights and work within the rhythms sellers are already used to.

When I spoke with Scott Jackson, Senior Director of Sales Enablement at Comcast Business, who shared his story with us in Chapter 3, he explained the importance of streamlining account planning within existing systems. "If your account planning software isn't embedded in your CRM, it's just impossible to sustain," he told me. "And it simultaneously increases the value of your CRM, because you get the relational context—I call it the three-dimensional view—into the people and politics of the account and the whitespace you might be missing."

---

7. **A trusted partner to ensure you succeed**

You're committed to your customers' success. You should get the same support from your vendors—particularly when the stakes are this high.

The company selling you your account planning software should serve as a partner who can guide you through the change-management process, commit to a regular cadence of success planning and business reviews, and help you deploy the software, train teams, operationalize and configure your processes, advise on best practices, and support you along your journey.

How can you maximize the return of your account planning software?

Bringing a new piece of technology to your sales team (and beyond) is tough, even on a good day. More than almost anyone else, sellers are focused on driving outcomes. Not to mention, their very livelihood may depend on their ability to successfully chase and win deals. Everything that makes them good at being salespeople can also make them less-than-ideal candidates when it comes to adopting a new piece of tech.

If salespeople so much catch a whiff of busy work, they'll be high-tailing it in the opposite direction.

Most sellers have good reason to be suspicious of new sales software. They've likely seen their fair share of self-proclaimed silver bullets that wound up being little more than yet another disconnected, glorified spreadsheet.

Sellers want to sell. Your account planning technology partner must ensure that your reps quickly and continually recognize the power of their new software to help them do just that.

Like account planning itself, you'll need buy-in from the entire sales organization to ensure success. And once you have your new tech in hand, change management, change execution programs, and ongoing support and services are vital.

How can you make sure sellers do more than log in and move on? There are *five* elements that maximize adoption:

---

1. **KPIs**

   What new behaviors do you expect from sellers?
   What adoption metrics are you looking to hit?
   Against what will managers be measured?

---

2. **Cadence**

   Build an operational rhythm for opportunity and account reviews (we'll cover what those look like in the next chapter) so that teams get comfortable in the tech and begin to see its power.

3. **Right-sizing**
    Help teams leverage different plan types and business rules that fit their activities and way of working.

4. **Coaching**
    Help sellers get comfortable and learn how to maximize their impact.

5. **Communication**
    Celebrate and socialize success. Show off early adopters and highlight big wins.

As a discipline, account planning is about organizing your internal teams around the success of your customers, creating mutual value, and breaking away from being considered "just another vendor."

Day-to-day, that means your teams must be working together to exchange information, create plans, and execute the actions required to make customers' goals a reality.

Technology is no substitute for the hard work of building relationships and creating real outcomes for your customers. But it is an essential tool. It forms the layer that connects your vision with your teams' actions.

The right software will allow you to optimize your team's performance on all levels from a single point of focus: your customer's success.

Outcome	Product Features
Collaboration	Central hub for sharing information between team members Actionable plans
Higher seller performance	In-app coaching, guidance, and reinforcement of best practices Actionable plans Adaptability for team-specific needs
Better relationships with customers	Insight maps Relationship maps
More pipeline and rigorous qualification	Relationship maps Visualization of deal progress Insight maps Visual whitespace analysis
Widespread adoption	Easy-to-use interface Adaptability Salesforce-native Change management support

> # "The purpose of a deal review is to help the salesperson see what they cannot see."

Tim Foster
Director, Growth Success,
Capita

12

Create a Winning Culture with Deal & Account Reviews

Tim Foster coaches revenue teams to success, winning over £1B of new revenue. As strategy advisor to CROs within FTSE 100 and fast-growth, high-tech unicorns, he is an expert on driving change. At Capita, Tim leads the marketing and bid teams that tell the Capita story and accelerate growth.

Without execution, a plan is nothing more than an idea.

Account planning, as we've discussed, is by definition a continuous process. There is no such thing as "set it and forget it." There is no box to be checked. As long as the opportunity is open and as long as you own the account, you are simultaneously susceptible to risk and within striking distance of reward.

That's where a regular cadence of deal and account reviews comes in.

Before we keep going, a quick note that reviews come in *two* forms:

---

1. **Deal reviews,** which assess the progress of a particular opportunity

2. **Account reviews,** which assess your position and potential within an account.

Though the two differ in scope (deal reviews are narrower, account reviews broader), they are grounded in the same principles and practices. In this chapter, we will primarily discuss the process of conducting deal reviews, but keep in mind that the same lessons can be applied to the exercise of running an account review. The difference comes down to your needs: advancing a specific deal or considering an account as a whole.

To get into the details of what makes reviews work and how you can run your own, I spoke with Tim Foster, the Director of Growth success at Capita. Tim has run hundreds of deal and account reviews, both for his own team and for his clients. He knows what works, what doesn't, and how to oversee a process that creates real business outcomes for both sales teams and their customers.

What do you risk without reviews?

When you forego a cadence of regular deal reviews, you leave sales progress vulnerable. "It is always what you don't know about a deal that ends up killing you."

Tim has seen the consequences up close.

In his work as an advisor, he took on a large print organization as a client. "They were a manufacturing giant," he remembers. Early in their relationship, Tim asked the CEO of the company what had driven him to take the leap to implement account planning software and best practices.

The CEO gave a heavy sigh.

His company, he explained, had been working on a huge bid with a Middle Eastern airline. It was going to be their biggest deal ever. They'd forecasted it and reported their expectations to the board. Everyone was delighted.

Until they weren't.

It was in the eleventh hour that they got the bad news: They'd lost the deal.

It had happened out of nowhere—a complete surprise. "And if there's one thing CEOs and CFOs hate," says Tim, "it's surprises. Because you can't manage surprises."

Dismayed, the CEO had been forced to return to the board and officially retract the forecast.

He told Tim: "I decided right then and there: We're never going to have a miss like that on our forecast again. We're never again going to invest the time and resources we did on a massive bid only to end up losing."

It was time, in other words, to banish surprises.

How might that story have played out differently with deal reviews? Would a review cadence have made a significant difference? Tim thinks so.

And he has good reason to feel confident in that assessment.

How can reviews transform a deal?

When the COVID-19 pandemic struck, Tim's team was knee-deep in an opportunity with a huge manufacturer. But as the stock market fell, offices closed, and companies around the world tightened their belts, the prevailing uncertainty and confusion spooked the middle managers with whom his reps were working. "It sent them into a state of paralysis," remembers Tim.

"We can't do this now," the contacts said. "We don't have the money. We'll probably need to wait at least six months. At that point, we can *maybe* do a pilot with 100 people."

A lesser leader might have shrugged it off and moved on. But from Tim's perspective, "It just didn't make sense." So he called a deal review.

"I pushed my team to really think about what was going on," he says. "And the clear recommendation that arose from the discussion was that we needed to test the thinking we'd heard from those middle managers we'd been talking to with the person in their organization who was actually responsible for the revenue number."

The team agreed. "We need to hear from that person and find out what they're going to do for the next year," decided the group. "Because, global crisis or not, they still have targets, and we can help them get there."

Getting higher up the corporate hierarchy was no easy task. It was two months before they reached him. The effort, though, was well worth it. "As it turned out, he had a completely different view than his middle managers did," said Tim.

"We've got to accelerate these programs," he told Tim's team. "The world has just gotten tougher and we still have numbers we need to hit. Everyone on my team is going to be at home for the foreseeable future, so we need to be able to enable them with tools and training without being together in the office."

Tim realized that this was the true compelling event his team needed. It had each one of the *three* key elements:

1. A clearly defined timeline
2. A quantifiable impact
3. An individual who feels the pain.

The deal, which at first had looked as though it would be a minor €20k pilot had, over the course of three short months, ballooned into a multi-million euro agreement.

"Without working through the details and giving the account executive the support and confidence to challenge it, that deal would not have happened," says Tim.

"Getting our heads together in a deal review session allowed us to unpack what we were hearing, challenge our assumptions by asking the right questions, and make an actionable plan to pursue a deal that would ultimately be better for us and our customer."

The Big Question:
How can you build a review process that creates real results?

"There are good reviews and there are bad reviews," says Tim. The trick, of course, is making sure yours are the good kind. "A good review is for the benefit of the seller, often the antithesis of what people have experienced in the normal war room environment."

A good review is designed so that everyone involved:

1. **Understands the plan**
   What are we doing?

2. **Tests the plan**
   Is this the best approach? Where are the risks in the current plan?

3. **Improves the plan**

   How will we move forward?

In many ways, deal and account reviews represent the cul-
mination of all of the account planning pillars we've covered
in detail in Part III.

A successful review requires:

- Rigorous qualification practices (Chapter 8)
- Group insights from integrated teams (Chapter 9)
- A clear understanding of who matters within a
  customer's organization (Chapter 10)
- Supportive account planning technology
  (Chapter 11).

It's the synthesis of each of these component parts that
make deal and account reviews so effective. When you can
uncover the right insights and collaborate to chart the best
go-forward strategy, you'll ensure your sellers are always set
up for the highest possible likelihood of success.

Seven foundations of a winning review culture

1. **Timing is everything**

   The first critical aspect of successful deal reviews doesn't
   actually have anything to do with the review itself. Rather,
   explains Tim, it's all about the timing.

   "The most important part of a deal review is when
   you do it. It must be done early." In other words, this is
   your chance to qualify before you get too deep. From the
   start, stakeholders need to agree that it's a deal you want
   to pursue in the first place. As we covered in Chapter 8,
   there are four critical questions to consider:

1. Is there an opportunity?
2. Can we compete?
3. Can we win?
4. Is it worth winning?

Answering these questions early on ensures your revenue team stays focused and avoids misplacing their limited attention.

---

2. Cadence is key

Reviews should be conducted regularly, built into the cadence of the sales team.

What exactly that cadence looks like may vary by team, but most successful account planning operations conduct reviews weekly, permanently setting aside time on Fridays to gather people together for productive discussion.

That's exactly what Anthony Reynolds, CEO of HireVue, does. "We do our forecast call on Monday morning and then the team has Monday afternoon, Tuesday, Wednesday, and Thursday to go be in front of customers. On Friday, we come back, and that's when we spend the time doing our account plan reviews. That cadence is critically important," he says.

The frequency with which you should be reviewing individual deals and accounts may depend on their health, status, size, and strategic significance.

- **Account plans** should be initially created in collaboration with the account team. Progress on critical objectives should be reviewed on a regular basis—generally once per month.

  Every quarter or every six months, depending on the size of the account, the team should gather to review the plan and reset any objectives that need to be updated.

- **Opportunity reviews** should be done at the early stages of the buying cycle and repeated whenever there is a significant change in the key players or the customer's landscape more broadly.

---

3. **It's an action plan, not a status update**

No one needs another pointless meeting.

"We call our review meetings 'Test & Improves,' and those terms are no accident," explains Tim. "This is not a briefing for management. It's not a meeting during which you get together to design the narrative of a forecast. No. The purpose of a deal review is to help the salesperson see what they cannot see."

Sellers, explains Tim, simply cannot work a deal alone. "When you're in the middle of a deal, you literally cannot see the wood for the trees."

Explaining the current state of the opportunity should be the jumping-off point, not the end goal. Instead of giving a presentation to an audience, a seller in a deal review should ultimately have a productive discussion with everyone in the room.

By the time a review is finished, the owner should:

- Know where their blind spots are
- Have practical recommendations for next steps
- Receive offers of support from stakeholders in taking those next steps.

"As a seller, you have to be involved in the details. But sometimes, the detail is not your friend," says Tim. "You have to have people help you take a step back and consider the wider picture."

4. **Outside voices matter**

One of the most important elements of a review is its guest list.

"Diversity of thought in any deal review process is really helpful," says Tim. "If you get five people in a room who all do the same job and have had the same sorts of conversations with the customer, you end up with group-think: you risk all thinking the same way and never challenging yourself."

In addition to bringing in people who interact with your customer from across the revenue team, like marketers, customer success managers, and more, you should also consider people from outside the traditional range of perspectives. "I often invite people from the engineering division," says Tim. "They always ask questions that are completely different from what anybody else asks because they just approach the problem from a totally different perspective."

Your group should also reflect the sorts of people involved in the process on the customer side. "Particularly when deals start to get complicated, you need to map your deal review process with your customer's decision process," Tim says. "If you think about the five or six key decision makers, who might oversee finance, data security compliance, enablement, whatever it may be—we need to understand what they're thinking. If you can get those voices in the room during a deal review, you'll have a much better understanding of how your customer is thinking."

5. **Inspire confidence, not fear**

You're reviewing the deal, not the seller.

"Particularly with large accounts or deals, sellers invest a great deal of time, effort, and emotion," says Tim. "And quite frankly, the outcome might have a major impact on their earnings. All of that means that salespeople often build up a shell of invincibility and confidence around them which makes being vulnerable and opening themselves to questions incredibly difficult."

Deal and account reviews should never serve to shame someone or put them on the spot to prove their progress. Rather, reviews should feel like safe places where reps can collaborate with a trusted team to work a problem, spot potential pitfalls, and identify opportunities to succeed.

"One sales leader I worked with once likened a deal review to a conversation with a critical friend who isn't personally involved and can be trusted to give you honest feedback," says Tim.

---

6. **Stick to the process**

"The thing that gets in the way of a good deal review is not actually having a process for it," says Tim.

Without predetermined steps and assigned roles, it's easy to end up wasting an hour on an unproductive discussion that goes in circles.

For that reason, it's useful to have a standard approach that gives everyone a clear understanding of what will happen, how long it will take, and what is expected from them.

---

7. **Support and scale the process with software.**

With structure being as important as it is, technology is an essential piece of infrastructure that can create guardrails and keep everyone on track. The right account planning software will help participants understand their roles, prompt people to take the necessary steps, and offer an easy way to collect, share, and visualize information.

Visualization is one of the most important pieces of the puzzle. When discussing key players within an account, for example, pulling up relationship maps can help participants get a sense of the account owner's foothold within the organization.

Integrated, easy-to-use software will ensure that all of the information about an account or a deal is up to date and can be easily shared with the team.

The three phases of a productive deal or account review

1. Present the plan
   Speaker: Account owner
   Goal: Share information

To start, it's all about the uninterrupted flow of information. The account owner has the floor to open the review, and their job is to get everyone in the room up to speed. To that end, they should report:

- The current state of the account or opportunity
- What they know
- What they don't know
- What's been done so far.

"People will be tempted to jump in," says Tim. "But the account owner should have the floor with no interruptions. This is one of the inflection points that define the success of the review. People have to make a difficult behavior change and learn to listen to the end without interjecting."

---

2. **Understand the plan**
    Speaker: Group
    Goal: Fill in information gaps

Here, the reviewers have the opportunity to clarify information they are unsure of. They should still be in information-gathering mode.

"This is a second critical point. None of these questions should make indirect comments on the quality of what the account owner presented," cautions Tim. "There should be no criticism; no suggestions of what people should do. The only goal should be to clarify any missing or unclear information."

What might that look like? "Quite often, the starting point is: 'Do we have a clear articulation of the compelling event? Do we know what terrible things are gonna happen if the customer doesn't act? Who is the individual that's really feeling the pain?'"

---

3. **Improve the plan**
    Speaker: Everyone
    Goal: Collaborate to find specific next steps

Now, as a group, the time for suggestions begins. Reviewers have the opportunity to point out vulnerabilities, risks, or blockers that might stop the deal from happening.

"The golden rule here is that you can only point out a vulnerability if you also come up with a *specific* recommendation for what the account owner should do about it," says Tim. "And if that person can actually help make that idea happen, well, even better."

Oftentimes, the most productive sessions arise when participants adopt specific roles and points of view. "One person can think about it from the customer's perspective, one from the purchasing manager, et cetera," explains Tim.

What happens next?

When the review is over, it's time to turn the discussion into action.

The seller and their manager should meet separately to consider the vulnerabilities and recommendations that surfaced in the group discussion and agree on which ones they want to undertake.

Then, it's time for the seller to speak with the customer.

"This is the critical part that many people avoid," says Tim. "You have to go back to the customer and find out the missing information. Whatever the recommendations are, the hardest and most impactful ones are going to involve taking your gaps to your customer."

"'Because this is such an important project both for you and for us, we got the team together to do a deep dive. We found some gaps in our understanding of your plan. Can you help me?'"

Customers are often more willing to part with that kind of information than you might think.

"If it's a real project that has real fire and pain behind it, your customer will give you the answers, share information, and introduce you to new people," Tim says. "If they don't want to discuss it, that might be a red flag that you're involved in an opportunity that doesn't have a compelling event."

Deal and account reviews bring together the fruits of account planning in a single, hyper-productive burst.

At their core, reviews rest on trust. Sales reps must feel confident in exposing their position and their vulnerabilities. Other members of the revenue team (and beyond) must be bought in on the power of collaborative insights. Everyone must understand the importance of qualification, influence, and of putting customer goals above all else. Technology must provide the backbone for information sharing, visualization, and the reinforcement of best practices.

With all these essential pieces in place, reviews are the ultimate way to live and breathe account planning as a revenue team, uniting forces to determine how you can make your customers as successful as possible.

"*Account planning needs to manifest itself everywhere the revenue team operates.*"

Anthony Reynolds
Chief Executive Officer,
HireVue

Conclusion
The Rise of the Revenue Team

Anthony A. Reynolds *is the Chief Executive Officer of HireVue. Reynolds brings over 20 years of leadership experience in enterprise SaaS, leading large cross-functional teams across multiple geographies.*

What makes some sales teams so good at what they do?

That's the question that opened this book, and it's the one we've spent the last dozen chapters considering.

The short answer is this: great sales teams prioritize the goals of their customers. In doing so, they're able to transform the quality and the depth of their relationships and throw off the yoke of being seen as "just another vendor."

The longer answer, as we've seen over the course of this book, is that they apply rigor, technology, and long-term thinking to this theory—in other words, they do account planning.

In some ways, though, we started our journey with a trick question.

Because it isn't sales teams that are great—at least not ones that operate alone.

The future of selling is collaborative

Account planning is the product of a collaboration, one that we call the revenue team. Beyond account managers and sales reps, it includes:

- Sales engineers
- Customer success managers
- Marketing teams
- Professional services
- Executives
- Subject-matter experts
- ...and more.

Whether you're qualifying a deal, researching for insights, building relationships with the people who matter, or keeping your progress on track with reviews, your sellers need the input and effort of people from across your organization who can all work together, speak the same language, and follow aligned processes to make big things happen.

Anthony Reynolds, CEO of HireVue, sees the revenue team as central to his account planning success. "The goal of good account planning is very simple: Find more pipeline; create more opportunities," he says. "But left to their own devices, a sales team will focus on selling opportunities and spend all their time there. A revenue team will step back and ask: 'How can we think bigger?'"

It's this kind of thinking that puts you in a position to become a trusted advisor.

"A trusted advisor is someone who understands their customer's industry and business problems," explains Anthony. "It's someone who knows the value they'll be able to provide because they've immersed themselves. This sort of seller doesn't ask: 'What's my strategy for the customer?' Instead, they ask: 'What's my customer's strategy and how can I help?' Understanding the problems your customer is trying to solve and helping them solve them is key to becoming a trusted advisor.

"When you involve the extended revenue team, you get access to people who spend a great deal of time understanding what your customers are doing and what challenges they're up against. Working together allows the conversations these folks are having to be a critical resource for the sales team to identify how they can best serve their customers."

Thus it's critical that we see the rise of account planning as the rise of the revenue team—the dismantling of silos that have previously divided customer interactions into isolated segments of a linear journey.

"Good teams hire people into positions who know how to execute in their swim lanes," says Anthony. "But great teams make passing the baton so fluid that it becomes invisible to the customer."

What possibilities does account planning unlock?

The evidence of the revenue team's impact is all around us, and we've seen it on these pages again and again.

Todd Adair, with whom we opened our story, began as a seller who had money coming in but who still lacked the deep trust of his customers.

In shifting his priorities from closing deals to building deep insights and helping his customers strategize for their future, he was able to transform his relationship. His success was so significant that it helped to spur the launch of GE Healthcare's Ascend sales program, which Todd joined full-time in order to bring these insights and processes to the team at large.

His transformative story is one of many.

- Jason Cooper's team began working together to share insights and doubled their win rate (Chapter 2)
- Sarah Walker's team collaborated to think bigger about how they engaged customers and grew the sector by two-thirds, doubled their win rate, and increased NPS by 100 points (Chapter 8)
- Tim Foster pushed his team to work together to assess the deal before them and flipped a small pilot into a multi-million euro deal (Chapter 12).

In being willing to ask tough questions, ask for help, and make themselves vulnerable, all of these leaders—along with the others profiled in this book—saw their worlds change for the better.

Where will account planning take you?

If helping our customers succeed is our ultimate objective, we can't afford to wall ourselves off from one another. Instead, Anthony says, "Account planning needs to manifest itself everywhere the revenue team operates."

As a sales leader, you will lead this charge.

Every hero in this book is a determined leader: someone with both big-picture vision and the grit to see that vision through. If you're reading this book, this is the role you are poised to play.

Great sales leaders recognize that account planning can't live within the confines of the sales department. They invest in building internal alliances and structures that bring people together and rally everyone around their customers.

In this new era, every member of the revenue team has a role to play in uncovering the customer's goals and aligning with the right people to help achieve them. It's your job to create the conditions that allow this coalition to thrive.

Great leaders also see that putting customers first isn't something you do once, and that account planning isn't a hack or a quick fix. It's something that embeds itself into your sales DNA. It becomes foundational to the way you approach your financial years, your quarters, and your days.

Making account planning the central pillar of the way your team operates will mean reorienting your organization as a whole and fixing their gaze on your customers' success.

As your relationships deepen and your numbers begin to climb, don't be surprised if your peers begin to wonder how your team is so exceptional at what they do.

If they ask, you can tell them: "We're not just another vendor."

www.ingramcontent.com/pod-product-compliance
Lightning Source LLC
Chambersburg PA
CBHW042116190326
41519CB00030B/7520